A Brief Sketch

OF THE

Settlement and Early History

OF

Giles County Tennessee

⤐⤏

James McCallum

Heritage Books
2024

HERITAGE BOOKS

AN IMPRINT OF HERITAGE BOOKS, INC.

Books, CDs, and more—Worldwide

For our listing of thousands of titles see our website
at
www.HeritageBooks.com

A Facsimile Reprint
Published 2024 by
HERITAGE BOOKS, INC.
Publishing Division
5810 Ruatan Street
Berwyn Heights, MD 20740

James McCallum
1876

Originally published by
The Pulaski Citizen
Pulaski, Tennessee
1928

International Standard Book Number
Paperbound: 978-0-7884-8984-6

FOREWORD

By W. B. Romine

On assuming the duties incident to editing and publishing the Pulaski Citizen in 1894, I soon realized the need for more information about the people among whom I had come to live and work.

By inquiry I learned that no history of the county had ever been published. But learned of the Centennial Address of Mr. McCallum, with additions which he had made to it, and that the manuscript had been filed with the State Historical Society at Nashville.

I engaged Lem A. Dever one of the first young men in town who had learned to operate a typewriter, paid him wages and expenses, to go to Nashville and make a copy of the manuscript for me.

Some twenty-five years later, a gentleman in Nashville, who wished to see the manuuscript, was referred to the Historical Society, when he found that the original had been lost or misplaced. It is fortunate for the County that I had a copy, for this manuscript contains much valuable information about the early settlers which could not now be replaced.

I have long cherished the hope that I may some day add to the History of the County as prepared by Mr McCallum and have accumulated memoranda, including incidents of the Civil War, and since that time. But as the years go by I find no more leisure. And feeling that the valuable work of Mr. Mc-Callum should be made accessible to the people, in the form in which he prepared it, and that he should have credit as its author, with the assistance and co-operation of Mike D. Sullivan, this little book is published in the hope that it may promote patriotic interest in those who have gone before, and who by their sacrifices, have prepared a better place for posterity.

In addition to the honors referred to by Col. Rose, I may add that Mr. McCallum served as Grand Master of Tennessee Masons. To those who understand, that will help to indicate the character of man he was.

FOREWORD

By Col. Solon E. Rose

To the President and Directors of the Tennessee Historical
    Society:

Gentlemen:

Hon. James McCallum, author of the "Early Settlement
and History of Giles County," owing to his feeble state of
health cannot present in person his MSS, and has requested
that I shall deliver it to the Tennessee Historical Society.

Mr. McCallum is more familiar with the past history of
Giles, than any other man now living, and although past
seventy years of age, was eminently qualified to perform the
task. He is a thorough scholar, a ready and terse writer, and
a "History of the Early Settlement of Giles County," is as
complete as the lapse of time would permit.

Mr. McCallum was long Clerk and Master in Chancery at
Pulaski, a member of the Legislature in 1861, a member of the
Confederate Congress, a citizen for more than seventy years
of Giles County; and long an active, practicing attorney in
the several courts of the State. These several positions, together with his peculiar adaptation, affords him facilities few
possessed to write this history. I should fail to discharge
the obligations of my mission if I did not testify on behalf of
our people to the social worth of James McCallum,—a Christian gentleman, a model in all the relations of life, who has
now the ardent admiration of all who have known him. His
broad sympathies, active charities, and social virtues are at-
tested by the warm friendship and admiration of his many
life-long friends; and now to a life of usefulness he has added
this additional service of transmitting this history to posterity.

Giles may have had more illustrious men, but none more
honored and beloved.

FOREWORD
By James McCallum

To the President and Directors of the Tennessee Historical
Society:

I have the honor of presenting to the Historical Society
of Tennessee, the following duplicate copy of a "Brief Sketch
of the Settlement and Early History of Giles County," with
the privilege of using the same or any part thereof in any
publication by the Society, reserving to myself the same right.

In the Summer of 1875, at the request of the Pulaski Lyceum, I collected a considerable amount of information, in
relation to the early settlement of the County, and, instead
of presenting it in the shape of a popular lecture, I read to
the Society such portions of it as I thought would be interesting.

In the Spring of 1876, at the request of the Committee on
the National Centennial, I collected further information on
the subject, and again only read such portions as I thought
would be appropriate to the occasion.

Believing that my information was too imperfect, and, in
some respect unreliable, to make History, I declined at the
time to publish it; I have since availed myself of all the
means in my power to add to the information and correct
errors.

Part First of the following transcript embraces substantially the information presented at the National Centennial, with
some slight corrections and additions.

Part Second embraces a description of the County, a history of our Courts, with the names and succession of our civil
and judicial officers, together with the names of our Senators
and Representatives both in the State and the National Legislature, intended to supply information, not otherwise accessible, from the loss of the Records of our Clerk's offices.

This has required no ordinary time, labor and expense
to accomplish. Altogether my transcript furnishes the material
to write a history, more than having claims to being a history
itself.

With the ardent wish that the Historical Society may
persevere in the laudable effort to rescue from oblivion the
unwritten history of our State, and transmit to posterity the
names, the adventures, and the noble deeds of the early settlers.

A BRIEF SKETCH OF THE SETTLEMENT AND EARLY HISTORY OF GILES COUNTY.

PART FIRST

Centennial Address, July 4th, 1876

There are epochs in the history of every country, characterized by a nobler type of humanity, than that which falls to the common lot of mankind; which leaves its impress on posterity.

Such was the era of our natal day, and of such were the great Statesmen and daring patriots, who, one hundred years ago, declared that the American Colonies owed no allegiance to the King of Great Britain, and boldly proclaimed the great political truth that "All Governments derive their just powers from the consent of the governed" And trusting to the God of Battles, threw down the wager to the Champion of the World. After several years of terrific warfare, they triumphed, and finally established a government upon the principles enunciated in their platform. The significance of the fundamental truth announced, and the establishment of a Government in accordance therewith, like a subterranean wave from a mighty volcano, shook all Europe, and extorted from the monarchies thereof written constitutions, or concessions, acknowledging in a greater or less degree, the rights of the people.

The virtues of those noble patroits were impressed in no section of the country more indelibly than on Tennessee.

She was born of the Revolution, baptized in its sufferings, "reared in times which tried men's souls." She came forth into the family of States as a trained athlete for victory and for honor. True to the inspiration of her early training, whenever duty has called or danger threatened, there her sons have been foremost, their blood has flown on every battlefield. Their valor has given renown to American arms, and won for them the proud appellation of the "Bravest of the brave."

Not alone on the battlefield has she won glory, but in the halls of legislation, in the forum, in the tribunals of justice, in the office of Chief Executive, her sons have stood the peers of the greatest and the best.

Giles County was the out-growth of those great principles The brave men and noble-hearted woman who were the first settlers of the County were the children of the Rvolution. And shall their names be forgotten? Shall no memorial be made of their adventures, their trials, and hardships, their energy, perseverance, and triumph? Shall no flower be dropped upon their graves, or rude stone mark their final resting place?

By request I propose to read you a "Brief Sketch of the Settlement and Early History of Giles County." It is known to most of you that at the request of the Pulaski Lyceum last year, I collected a considerable amount of information on the subject which would require more time to read, than is allowed me on this occasion. The brief sketch now offered emrbaces only a few of the names, and some of the most prominent features in the character of the first settlers.

Imperfect, as it may be, and, perhaps, in some of its details inaccurate, it is presented with the sincere desire to contribute something to rescue from oblivion the memory of those noble pioneers, to whom our country owes such a debt of gratitude. And with the hope that this humble effort will awaken inquiry, and call forth much that has not been within my reach.

To trace the development of those principles which animated the first settlers of our County, and ascertain the dominant idea with them to what they owed their success, and to note the changes and the wonderful progress that has been made, would be appropriate on the present occasion; but I do not propose to give a continuous history of the County. I shall confine myself chiefly to the settlement and early history of it, leaving to a future occasion, and to some other person, the less difficult and more pleasing task of showing the progress that has been made, with appropriate notices of the many useful and patriotic citizens that have passed away.

CHAPTER FIRST—CONDITION OF THE COUNTRY

To fully appreciate the character and noble achievements of those heroic men and women who came to the County when the whole face of the country was a dense cane-brake, inhabited only by wild beasts of the forest, with the Indians living in near proximity, and occasionally passing through it on their hunting or marauding excursions, it is necessary to recur to the antecedent and contemporaneous history of the country.

For this digression I ask your indulgence; it will doubtless be uninteresting to a portion of you, but to the youth who may be present, it may be necessary, to give them a just conception of the trials and difficulties the first settlers had to encounter.

Prior to the Revolutionary War, the British Government claimed the title in fee simple to all the lands in her American possessions not disposed of by the King, vested in him, and that the Indians were but tenants at will.

The Colony of North Carolina claimed that, under her Colonial Grant from the King, her boundaries extended West as far as the British Government had title, and, without admitting the title of the Indians, but from motives of policy, treated with them from time to time for portions of the land.

At that time and for many years before no Indians permanently resided within the State of Tennessee, except the southern portion of East Tennessee.

INDIANS

The Cherokees lived in North Georgia, the Southern part of East Tennessee, and South-western North Carolina, but claimed as hunting grounds East Tennessee, and Middle Tennessee, also Kentucky, and as far north as the Ohio River.

The Chickasaws occupied North and West Mississippi, the North-west part of Alabama, and the South bank of the Tennessee river, as far East as above Ditto's landing; and claimed as hunting grounds Middle and West Tennessee, and North Alabama; as far East as the head-waters of Duck and Elk Rivers, and North to the Cumberland and its tributaries.

The Creeks occupied the greater portion of Central and Eastern Alabama; the Middle and Western part of Georgia, and claimed the right to hunt in Middle Tennessee.

The Choctaws occupied Central and Eastern Mississippi, and Western Alabama; and claimed the right to hunt in Middle and West Tennessee.

The Shawnees lived on the Wabash, the Six Nations on

the Miami and Scioto, and the Westen Confederacy, consisting of about twenty nations, lived North of the Ohio, and West of the Six Nations. These all claimed the right to hunt on the Cumberland.

Th Indians had their trails and war paths through Tennessee, which they traveled in their hunting and war excursions from the settlements South of the Tennessee River, and those North of the Ohio

One of these, the old McCutcheon trail, crossed Elk River at Latitude Hill, passed through the Eastern portion of Giles crossed Duck River near the mouth of Fountain Creek, and North to the neighborhood of Nashville. Another crossed Elk River at the mouth of Ford's Creek near Prospect, and went North or North-west and was traveled in their excursions to Northern tribes.

The country between the Tennessee and Ohio Rivers had been for many years the great battle ground of the Indians, each Nation claiming an interest in it, but no one of them was permitted by the others to permanently occupy it; hence the vindictive and unceasing warfare they waged against the first settlers.

CHAPTER SECOND—INDIAN TREATIES

A permanent settlement having been effected on the Cumberland in 1779 or 1780 by General James Robertson and others, the General Assembly of North Carolina in 1783, established the County of Davidson, embracing the territory included in the district set apart to the officers and soldiers, and East to the Cumberland mountains, although the Indians at that time claimed all the territory in the County.

Without referring to the various treaties with the Indians, it is sufficient for our present purpose to state that in November, 1785, the Cherokees ceded their claim to the land North of the Ridge which divides the waters of the Cumberland from those of Duck, and and Eastwards to where a North-east line would strike the Cumberland forty miles above Nashville, thence with the river to where the Kentucky line crosses it, thence to Campbell's line near Cumberland Gap. In January, 1786, the Chickasaws ceded their claim to land North of said line. The Indian boundary as thus estab-

lished, remained such until January 1806, except the portion
which lies North of Duck River, as to which the Indian title
was extinguished in October 1805, and no person was permitted to settle South of that line.

Emigrants from the Eastern States came by way of Cumberland Gap or down the Ohio, and up the Cumberland.

In 1801 the United States Government opened a road
from Nashville to Natchez, called to Natchez road, which
crossed Duck River at Gordon's Ferry, below Williamsport,
and the Tennessee at Colburt's Ferry. The road from Williamson County was through Chickasaw territory the most of the
way, and they claimed the right to establish ferries, and houses of entertainment, on the road. There was then no white
family on the road from Gordon's Ferry to near Natchez.

In July, 1805, a treaty was made with the Chickasaws by
General Robertson and Colonel Meigs, by which they ceded
all their claims to land North of Duck River, and East of the
Natchez Road as far as the ridge that divides the waters of
Duck River from those of Buffalo, at Grinder's Station, twen-
ty-three miles South of Duck River, at present known as
"Lewis's Grave," and all North and East from a line from
Lewis's Grave eastwardly along said ridge to the headwaters
of the Buffalo, thence South-east to Ditto's landing,—striking
the Tennessee River three miles below the landing, and eight
miles below the Eastern boundary of the Chickasaw clain.
This line passed through Giles, entering it near the North-
west corner, crossing the Lawrenceburg road at the eight-
mile post, near where Robert Reed lived, passed four or five
miles West of Pulaski, crossed Elk River about three miles
above Prospect just West of the Ward place, and the State
Line at Phillips's Mill, the place known as "Old Virginia," and
then to Ditto's landing or near that on the Tennessee, leaving
a considerable part of the Western and South-western portion of Giles County in Chickasaw territory; and such it remained until the treaty of 1816, when the Chickasaws ceded
all their land North and East of the Tennessee River. In
October, 1805, the Cherokees ceded their claim to land North
of Duck River, and to the headwaters of the most Southern
branch, then Eastwardly to the mouth of the Hiawassee on
the Tennessee River.

In January, 1806, the Cherokees ceded all their claim to lands North of the Tennessee River, and West of the line run from upper part of Chickasaw "Old Fields" on the Tennessee River, about five miles above Ditto's landing, to the most eastwardly headwaters of Duck river, etc.

This treaty not being entirely satisfactory was reaffirmed by a subsequent treaty in September, 1807, including the headwaters of Elk River.

CHAPTER THREE—ORGANIZATION OF GILES COUNTY

Prior to 1806, many persons from the Eastern States, who had entered land in Middle Tennessee, South of Williamson County, moved to Davidson and Williamson, and resided there temporarily, waiting for the Indian title to be extinguished, that they might settle on their own land.

Williamson County was established in October, 1799, and its boundaries extended South to the Indian boundary, and all South of that was in Indian territory until after the treaty of January, 1806, except the portion which lies North of Duck River as to which, the Indian title was extinguished in October, 1805. Until after the organization of Maury County, what is now Giles County was regarded as a part of Williamson. Some of the old deeds and grants for lands in Giles County on the South side of Elk River, described the land as being in Williamson County, and were required to be registered there.

Maury County was established in November, 1807.

The territory South of Maury remained for two years under the jurisdiction of Maury. The first settlers paid taxes in Maury, prosecuted criminals, and instituted legal proceedings in the courts of Maury.

On the fourteenth of November, 1809, Giles County was established by act of the Legislature. The Bill was introduced by Wm. Frierson, grandfather of Judge W. F. Cooper, and uncle of Chancellor Flemming, the Representative of Williamson and Maury, to establish a new County South of Maury, and North of the State Line, by the name of "Richland County." The tradition is, that at the suggestion of General Jackson, "Giles" was substituted as the name of the County in honor of Governor William B. Giles, of Virginia. When the

Bill was on its third reading in the Senate, on motion of Mr. Benton, it was amended by striking out Giles, and inserting Shelby, as the name of the County. The House refused to concur in the amendment, and after some delay the Bill was finally passed, retaining the name Giles.

The boundaries of the County as defined by the Legislature, commenced at the South-east corner of Maury, thence South to the Southern boundary of the State, thence West far enough to include a constitutional County, thence North to the Maury line, thence with the Maury line to the beginning. As this indicated, nearly half of the County lay West of the Congressional Reservation line. The vacant land West of said line belonged to the United States Government, over which the State of Tennessee had no control, and about one-fourth of the County; the Western and South-western part, was Indian territory, and remained such until September, 1816.

The Act establishing the County appointed James Ross, Nathaniel Moody, Tyree Rodes, Gabriel Bumpass and Thomas Whitson, Commissioners, to select a place on Richland Creek, as near the center of the County as practicable, and cause a town to be laid off; and to sell lots, reserving a public square of two acres, on which should be erected a court house and stocks; that the Town should be called "Pulaski," in honor of Count Pulaski, who fell in the attack upon Savannah in 1779.

The Commissioners were judiciously selected as to their location. Ross lived at the Andrew Yokley place; Moody near Lynnville Station; Rodees where his son, Robert Rodes lived afterwards; Bumpass at Cross Water; and Whitson on Elk River, about a mile above Prospect on what was then Indian territory.

The Commissioners selected the present site of Pulaski, then known as the "Shoals on Richland Creek," although at that time it was vacant land, lying South and West of the reservation line, but assurance of title had been given, which authorized the Commissioners to make the selection. The cane and undergrowth were removed from a small portion of the town in 1810. Among those who removed the first cane were: General R. H. Allen, then a lad fifteen years of age, and Spencer Clack, then a young man living with his father, one mile West of the court house.

In August, 1811, the first lots were sold, and in due time a court house and stocks were erected.

On the twenty-second of November, 1809, the Legislature, by joint resolution, selected the following magistrates for Giles County, viz: John Dickey, Jacob Baylor, Somerset Moore, Charles Neely, Robert Steele, Nathaniel Moody, William Phillips, Benjamin Long, Thos. Westmoreland, David Porter and Maximillian H. Buchanan. At the same time the Legislature elected Thos. Stewart, Judge of the Fourth Distrist, embracing Giles and Alfred Balch, Attorney General.

Dickey lived at Campbellsville, Baylor one mile West of it, Moore on Moore's Creek, two miles South-west of Pulaski, Neely on Pigeon Roost Creek, near the Tillery place, Steele on the turnpike, opposite Buford Station, Moody half a mile South of Lynnville Station, Phillips two miles North of Elkton, Long in the suburbs of Elkton, Westmoreland near Aspen Hill, Porter near Mout Moriah Church, and Buchanan at Crosswater.

The Act which established the County also established a Circuti Court, to be held the second Monday in June and December; and a Court of Pleas and Quarter Sessions, to be held third Monday in February, May, August and November; and provided that the first courts should be held at the house of Lewis Kirk, who lived in a log cabin on the bank of Richland Creek, about two hundred yards above the Nashville and Decatur Depot.

The first County Court was held third Monday in February, 1810, when the Magistrates were sworn in, and County officers elected or appointed. German Lester was made Clerk, Charles Neely, Sheriff, ———————, Chairman and Jesse Westmoreland, Register. Charles Neely, the first sheriff, was one of the Magistrates, and the tradition is that the magistrates, at the first election for sheriff, wre in favor of keeping the office among themselves, as was the custom in the State of Virginia at that time; but, owing to some dissatisfaction about the mode of electing, Neely resigned and James Buford, who was his deputy, was elected.

The third Circuit Court was held in June, 1810. Thomas Stewart was Judge, and James Berry was appointed Clerk.

The first courts of the County were attended by a large number of attorneys from other counties, among them were: Thomas H. Benton, Felix Grundy, O. B. Hays, Alfred Balch, Marmaduke Williams, Peter R. Booker, John Kelly, John White, Robert Mack, Wm. White, Easthouse Lewis, ———— Haskell, Coulter, and others; besides Alfred M. Harris, George Cunningham and Lunsford M. Bramlette, resident attorneys. A few years later Aaron V. Brown, Wm. H. Field and Tryon M. Yancey were numbered with the resident lawyers. At a later date, John H. Rivers, Wm. C. Flournoy, Collin S. Tarpley, E. J. Shields, James W. Coombs,—and a few years later, Archibald Wright, Neill S. Brown, Calvin Jones, John W. Goode, Thomas M. Jones, A. F. Goff, and Dixon Topp, were added to the number of resident attorneys. Thos. H. Benton was attorney for the Plaintiffs in the first two cases on the Civil Docket in the Circuit Court. Henry Clay's name appears on the docket as an attorney at three or four courts a few years after the courts were organized. It is said he was looking after an important land suit.

On the twenty-third of November, 1809, the Legislature chartered an Academy for Giles County, called Pulaski Academy, and appointed John Sappington, Nelson Patterson, Tyree Rodes, Samuel Jones, Somerset Moore, Charles Buford, and Charles Neely, Trustees; and in the month of September, 1812, the name of the Academy was changed to Wurtemburg Academy; and Doctor William Purnell, David Woods, and Alfred M. Harris appointed additional Trustees

In 1809, the Legislature declared Richland Creek navigable to the mouth of Big Creek. A few years later the Act was so amended as to declare it navigable only to Pulaski; after which a mill was built on the creek at Pulaski, and another below Mt. Moriah Church.

In the Legislature of 1809, Thos. H. Benton represented the Counties of Williamson, Rutherford, Bedford, and Maury, in the Senate; and William Frierson, Williamson and Maury in the House of Representatives. In the Legislature of 1811, Amos Johnson represented Williamson, Maury and Giles in the House; Newton Cannon represented Williamson, Rutherford, Maury, Bedford, Lincoln and Giles in the Senate.

CHAPTER FOUR—FIRST SETTLERS

The first white persons who explored Giles County or passed through it, so far as is now known, were the Commissioners with their guard, and citizens who accompanied them to lay off a district on the Northern part of Middle Tennessee, 55 miles wide, for the satisfaction of warrants issued by the State of North Carolina to her officers and soldiers; and to lay off a tract of twenty-five thousand acres South of that district, donated to General Greene.

A large number of those who went out in said expedition went across the State from Nashville, through the Eastern portion of the County to Latitude Hill on Elk River, and on their return passed up Indian Creek, over to and up Buchanan's Creek; and thence to Fountain Creek in Maury County. After that time and until 1790, it was occasionally visited by locators and surveyors in search of land. The entering of land being stopped by the United States Government as soon as the cession of the territory was accepted, but few persons came to the County until after the Indian tile was extinguished. Although a large portion of the best lands in Giles County was located and entered soon after the passage of the Act in 1783, and grants issued for a considerable portion of it, yet the owners were not permitted to go upon their lands, or to have them surveyed or the lines marked, until after the treaty of January, 1806. And until after that time it is believed there were no permanent settlements in the County.

It is now very difficult to ascertain who were the first settlers and when they came. But few of the first settlers who were old enough to remember dates when they came are now living.

I have met with a few who think their parents were in the County in 1805, others in 1806, and that corn was raised in the County in those years; but upon inquiry as to who came with them, or who were here before them, or came the same year they did, or the rotes they came, I am inclined to believe they are mistaken as to dates.

It is highly probable there were a few here in 1806, and possibly in 1805, as we find adventurers on Indian lands in other places, notwithstanding the prohibition of the Government. But who they were, or when they came, if any such were here, I have not been able to satisfactorily ascertain.

The information upon which I base the following account of the early settlement of the County, has been derived from the few of the early settlers yet living, who were young men and women when they came; from those who were of an age to remember how old they were when their parents came, and from those who learned from their parents how old they were at the time they came, or that they were born the year before or the year after they came verified by family records. From these and from the records of the County, together with what I learned from my parents who came to the County in 1809 when I was a small boy; and from what I learned from other old settlers having had a general acquaintance throughout the County since early manhood, I believe the persons hereinafter named were among the first settlers and that they came about the dates mentioned. Many others, whose names are not mentioned, were early settlers, but I have been unable to learn when they came.

It is believed that the first permanent settlement in the County was made on Elk River near the mouth of Richland Creek; and in the neighborhood of Prospect by emigrants from East Tennessee who came down the Tennessee River in boats to the mouth of the Elk, and thence up Elk.

The treaties of 1805 and 1806 extinguished the Indian title to a considerable portion of what is now Madison County, in Alabama, a scope of country in the shape of a "V," some thirty miles wide on the South boundary of the Tennessee with a point on the Tennessee River at Ditto's landing, with about eight miles front on the river. Soon after the treaty, Zacharia Cox and his associates, the "Tennessee Zazoo Company," claimed this scope of country as against the U. S. Government. Under their purchase from the State of Georgia in 1795, and commenced settling it and having it settled up.

They were resisted by the Government and those claiming under said purchase were driven off. But the character of the country being well known to the people of East Tennessee, soon after the treaty a number of persons of wealth and influence came down the river in boats and settled around what is called Hunt's Spring, afterwards Huntsville; and soon thereafterwards, others descended the river to the mouth of the Elk, and ascended Elk to the neighborhood of Prospect, and the mouth of Richland. Among these were William Crowson and his four sons, and his son-in-law, Vincent, with their families, who came about February, 1807, and settled the West side of Richland Creek, and near the mouth of it, and raised corn in 1807.

About the same time or soon thereafter, Thos. Whitson, settled on Whitson's Creek, a mile or two above Prospect, and for him the creek was named. Reynolds settled on the placed owned by Thos. Reed, Esq., at the time of his death, and for him Reyonlds' Island was called. Jordan Ward settled on the north bank of the river three miles above Prospect, at what has since been known as the Abel Ezell place. A man named Jenkins settled on Jenkins' Creek, for whom the creek was named. A man named Johnson between Ford's and the Thomas Reed place; and a man named Ellis settled near the Reed place; a family named Easley settled on the south side of the river, opposite the mouth of Richland, near where John Bailey lives.

These settlers with a few others in the neighborhood raised corn in 1807. James Ford with a number of others, including James Williams, Parish Simms, Thos. Dodd, Simon Foy, and Thos. Kyle, with their families started from Hawkins County in East Tennessee in the Spring of 1807 with four boats, when the boats had ascended Elk about opposite Simms' settlement three of the boats with the Simmses, Kyle and others went out to view the country, and concluded to stop there and sttled what was lonk known as Simm's settlement, in Limestone County, Ala.

Ford with his boat and those with him ascended the river some distance and stopped and with a canoe, Ford and two or three men went up the river several miles until they came to a small branch running into the river a short distance above the mouth of Ford's Creek, when they stopped, and, as they landed Ford said, "Boys, this is my spring branch," and going up the branch they soon found the spring.

Ford went back and brought up his boat, and landed on the north side of the river at the mouth of the spring branch, about 200 yards above the railroad bridge, on the fourth day of June, 1807 He built a house near the spring. The place has since been know as the Dever place, and is now owned by A. J. Reed, Esquire, and adjoins Prospect on the East. Ford's Creek that runs by Prospect, was named from Ford.

Two or three months after Ford came, Major Wm. Kyle came and settled on the south side of the river, opposite Prospect, at what has since been known as the Brown or Veto place. He was a man of considerable property, and owned a number of slaves. About the same time the McKinneys came and settled in the neighborhood. The old man Hunnicut and sons came soon after Ford and settled on the south side of the river below the mouth of Richland; the place is now owned by the heirs of Daly. John Tucker came the same year and settled the Tucker place now owned by Carey Gilbert, Esquire. James and Wm. Price, came about 1808 and settled on the East side of Richland Creek near the mouth at what was called "Lower Elkton." John and Lewis Nelson came about 1809 and settled a few miles North-east of Prospect. John Nelson settled where his widow now lives, and Lewis Nelson in the same neighborhood. Dr. Gabriel Bumpass, with a number of families from South Carolina, settled at Crosswater at a very early date. The precise date cannot be ascertained; but from the fact that the Bufords and others traveled his trail as early as the Fall of 1807, he must have come sometime in 1807 as early at least as the Summer or Fall.

In the party that came with Bumpass were William Buchanan and his sons Robert, Maxmillian H., (the father of Mrs. Col. Solon E. Rose), John and Jesse, Timothy Ezell, Mike Ezell and William Ezell, the father of P. H. Ezell, together with others whose names are not remembered. Dr. Bumpass settled the Crosswater place now owned by George E. Suttle, Wm. Buchanan settled the place owned by the Reverened C. P. Reed; Robert Buchanan about a half mile North of where Reed lived on the east side of Buchanan's Creek; it is not certainly known whether the creek took its name from them, or was named by the Commissioners in 1783, as there was a Buchanan with them. The general impression is that it took its name from Robert Buchanan who lived on it and built a mill on it about 1809; it was grinding in 1810. The Ezells settle east of the mill, and in the immediate neighborhood.

Bumpass and his company opened the first road in the

County South from Columbia; it came to Little Bigby by where Pillow's Mill was, striking the Giles County line at what is now known as Yokley's Gap, at the headwaters of what is now known as the eastern branch of Big Creek and down the same by Cunningham's, now John English's; thence by Andrew Yokley's, thence a little East of Campbellsville, by the place John I. Morris lives on, thence South on the dividing ridge between Big Creek and little Dry Creek striking Dry Creek where Sam Wilson lives; crossing Weakley Creek at Reed's ford, near the South-east corner of . Reed's land; thence up Agnew Creek, thence by the Walthall place, known as the William D. Abernathy place; thence to Coopertown, and by the Black place to Richland, crossing at Mrs. Tyree Rodes' farm, and thence to Crosswater, making a very circuitous route to avoid the large cane. The cane was small on the ridges, and poor land, but very heavy in the creek bottoms, and on the rich land. This was called Bumpass's trail, and was the principal road for emigrants going as far South as Pulaski, and West of Pulaski—for two or three years. The first mails were carried on this route. Bumpass, the Buchanans, Ezells, and others, who came about the time they did, raised corn in 1808. Lewis Brown, Lester Morris, Buckner Harwell and his sons, William Crittendn and his sons, Alexander Tarpley, Robert McNairy, William Wells, Sr., and his sons, Mark Mitchell, Jesse Westmoreland, Thos. Westmoreland, W. B. Pepper, Colonel L. Cleaveland, Reverend William Calloway and William Abernathy, (father of Chas. C. Abernathy,) came in the latter part of 1808, and early in 1809. They all or the most of them made corn in 1809. Cleaveland and Calloway may have made corn in 1808. The Westmorelands lived in Davidson County, sent their hands out, and improved places and made crops, but did not move their families out until the latter part of 1809.

Lewis Brown settled on Richland Creek on the place known as the Ira Brown place. Lester Morris was a Revolutionary soldier and settled about a half mile West of Rehoboth Churc; Buckner Harwell, Sr., settled the farm now owned by John Marks, and his sons settled in the neighborhood. His son, Colonel Gilliam Harwell, father of Dr. T. B. Harwell, settled not far from where Dr. Harwell now lives. William

Crittenden settled the place lately owned by Robert Dickson. Robrt McNairy, Alex Tarpley, and Wm. B. Pepper, settled the places on which they resided at the time of their deaths, and which have been long known by their names. Mark Mitchell sttled the place now owned by Colston Abernathy; Jesse Westmoreland settled the place now owned by John Newbill; William Wells the place since known as the Wells or Moseley place; Cleaveland and Calloway settled on the old Stage Road, half a mile or three quarters south of where the Reverend C. P. Reed lived. Cleaveland at the place Birdsong lived on, and Calloway about 300 yards further on South. Calloway was a Baptist preacher, and one of the first preachers in the County Wm. Abernathy settled the place Chas. C. Abernathy now lives on. He sent his hands out from Davidson County, improved the place and made a crop, but did not move out his family until the latter part of the year. One of the first churches in the County was a Baptist Church about a quarter of a mile South of or South-west from Crosswater spring, built in 1809 by the Buchanans and Ezells. Rev. George Brown and perhaps, Calloway were the preachers. A Methodist Church at Rehoboth was built in 1810, principally by Lewis Brown, who was a man of considerable property.

Lewis Brown erected a horse mill about 1810, which was resorted to from a considerable distance in the Summer season. Dr. Bumpass practiced medicine at Crosswater; and over a large extent of country,—as there were but few physicians in the county. He was a learned and skillful physician, but a man of great eccentricity of character so much so that his influence was effected by it. Among those who came at later date to the neighborhood of Crosswater were: Robert Oliver, who lived for many years on the place afterwards owned by the Reverend C. P. Reed and Isaac Mason who settled on the place long known as the Mason place, and Thos. Meredith, who setled the place where Mrs. Tyree Rodes now lives.

SECTION THREE—ASPEN HILL AND NEIGHBORHOOD

The neighborhood of Aspen Hill was settled at a very early date. Thomas Reed, Sr., the father of the late Thomas Reed, Esq., came from Kentucky and settled the place Thomas Reed, Esquire, first lived on, about a quarter of a mile East of where J. P. C. Reed now lives.

Old William Riggs, Joseph Moore, and Daniel Cox, came about the same time. Dan Cox settled on Richland Creek, where Thomas Westmoreland a year afterwards settled, long known as the Jones place. James Kimbrough, the father of Henry T. Kimbrough, Elijah Anthony and Joseph Anthony, the father of James D., and Joseph C. Anthony all came about the same time and settled in the neighborhood. Joseph Anthony, whre James D., now lives. Joseph C. Anthony, thinks his father came about 1805; and J. P. C Reed thinks his grandfather came about 1806, but as they have no record of dates to refer to, and as they nearly all came along the Bumpass trail, it is very probable they came in the Summer or Fall of 1807. They all raised corn in 1808. In the latter part of 1808, or first of 1809, Thomas Westmoreland, father of the late Thos. A. Westmoreland, Esq., brought out his servants and settled on what has since been called the Jnoes place.

He made a crop in 1809, and moved his family out from Davidson County in the latter part of 1809. He was appointed by the Legislature in the Fall of 1809, one of the first Justices of the Peace in the County, and must have been regarded as a citizen of the County at that time. John Butler and John Barnett came soon after Westmorelands; the precise date not known. Butler settled on what was long known as the Butler place, North of Aspen Hill. Barnett settled about a mile South-west of Aspen Hill. A few years later the Reverend Aaron Brown and his sons, Thomas and William settled in the neighborhood. The Reverend Aaron Brown on the place afterwards owned by his son, Governor Aaron V. Brown, and called the Aspen Hill place. Thos. Brown half a mile Southeast of Aspen Hill, at what has since been known as the Petty place. Wm. Brown at what has since been called the Steven Biles place. Captain Baker P. Potts settled at an early date West of the place owned by Governor Aaron V. Brown.

SECTION FOUR—PULASKI AND VICINITY

It is difficult to ascertain who were the first settlers in the town of Pulaski, or the date at which they came. It is believed, however, that Lewis Kirk, Alexander Black and his brother, Robert Black, were the first who lived in the town;

and that they came as early as the Fall or Summer of 1807. It
is known that they were here in 1807; settled the lot on which
David S. Martin now lives in First Main Street; Robert on the
same street near the old cemetery; Lewis Kirk on the bluff
at the foot of the shoals on Richland Creek, about two hundred yards above the Nashville and Decatur Depot. These
lots are now owned by Thos. Flippen and Pleasant Smith.
About the time the Blacks and Kirks came, or son after,
Ralph Graves, Sr., settled about two hundred yards East of
J. B. Childers's residence, and a little East of the Corporation
line. Charles Buford, Jas. Buford and Somerset Moore came
to the neighborhood of Pulaski in the Fall of 1807. The father of the Bufords, James Buford, Sr., was one of the first
settlers of Williamson County, lived in Williamson County
near Thompsons' Station and owned a tract of two thousand
acres of land adjoining the South-west corner of Pulaski. His
sons and Moore who was a son-in-law, made some improvements on the land in 1807. In the Fall sowed turnips and
went back and moved their families out early in 1808. Charles
Buford settled the place known as the Charles Buford place.
James Buford the place now owned by the heirs of Nicholas
Buford; Somerset Moore the place on Moore's Creek, now
owned by Mrs. Fogg. The creek was named for him, though
Buford's and Moore came the Bumpass trail. Major John
Clack, with his son, Spencer Clack, moved from Sevier County, East Tennessee, and settled about a mile West of the
Court House on the Carter farm near where his negro cabins
were, early in 1808. These all raised corn in 1808. Wm. Gideon
came in 1808, and settled what was long known as the Gideon
place, on the Gideon road half a mile North of town. Col.
Nelson Patterson with his sons, James and Bernard M., came
in the latter part of 1808, and settled the Patterson place one
mile East of Pulaski. They raised corn in 1808. Major Thos.
Wilkerson, father of the late F. H. Wilkerson, came in 1809
and settled near the Patterson spring, between the spring and
Colonel Solon E. Rose's residence. Tyree Rodes sttled the
place his son, Robert Rodes now owns in 1809, probably in
the early part of the year. He was appointed by the Legislature in November, 1809, one of the Commissioners to lay off
the town of Pulaski. Wm Kerley, known as Captain Kerley

came to the County with him, and lived on his farm several years. Charles Neely settled near the Tillery spring, three miles North of Pulaski at a very early day; he was appointed by the Legislature in 1809 one of the magistrates of the County, and in February, 1810, was elected sheriff; John White, father of Dr. R. G. P. White, Newton and John M. White, settled the place Newton White lived on in the latter part of 1809 Wm. Mayfield and sons, were very early settlers, but the date they came is not known.

Steele, the father of the Alexander G. Steele and his sons were very early settlers. They settled the place now owned by the Honorable Thomas M. Jomes, two miles West of Pulaski on the Lawrenceburg road. Silas Flournoy, the grandfather of Capt. Wm. C. Flournoy, came about 1813, and settled on the Locust Hill place, where he died and was buried. Of the first settlers in the town, besides Kirk and the Blacks the following persons were here at a very early date, before 1812, but the date at which they came is not known.

Wm. R. Davis, Wm. Ball, Jas. Berry, German and Fountain Lester, Dan Martin, Richard Scott, Jas. Drew, Jas. H. Williams, Wm. Hamby, Thos. Smith, Jno. McCracken, Jno. Q. Talbot, Henry Hogan, Dr. Shadrack Nye, Joseph H. Trotter, Joseph H. Hodge, Dr. Gilbert D. Taylor, David Woods, Lewis James and William Conor, Samuel G. Anderson, Nathaniel Moody, Alfred M. Harris, Lunsford M. Bramlette, of these Davis, Ball, Scott, and Talbot were among the first. German Lester came in 1809; probably the latter part of the year. The Couny was established in November, 1809, the first County Court being held the third Monday in February 1810, when he was elected clerk of the County Court. The Town of Pulaski was located by the Commissioners and partly laid off some time in 1810, date not exactly known, but probably in the first half of the year as a commencement had been made to remove the cane from the public square before October, 1810; the first sale of lots was in August, 1811. Dr. Taylor came in 1811, and was here at the sale of the lots; the most of those named were here at the sale of the lots; some of them a year or two before. Bramlette, and perhaps a few others, did not come before 1812 or 1813. C. C. Abernathy, who first visited Pulaski, eleventh of October, 1810, and has lived in the immediate neighborhood ever since, thus describes the place. "The town had been located and partially laid off, and a few rods of cane had been cut down on the public square North of the present Court House, the balance of the public square and what is now the town was covered with tall cane; and large poplar, beech, and other forest trees.

Alexander Black lived in a log cabin near where David S. Martin now lives on First Main Street, and had cut down a few rods of cane where his house stood. Robert Black lived in a similar cabin, on the same street, near the old cemetery. Lewis Kirk lived in a rough log cabin on the bluff of Richland Creek at the foot of the shoals. A rough log house had been erected in his yard in which to hold court. Kirk kept a boarding house, and tavern during the session of the courts. Richard Scott had a small stock of goods in a cabin near Kirk's which he soon after sold out to Jno. Q. Talbot. William Ball kept a grocery in a cabin near Kirk's. These were then the only houses and improvements in what is now the Town of Pulaski that he remembered." A number of persons were then living in the immediate neighborhood and vicinity of whom he remembers, Patterson, Wilkerson, Black, the Bufords, Moore, and others. Mr. Abernathy further states that after some of the lots were sold in August, 1811, and the cane cut down on the public sqquare, a court house was built on the public square out of round logs and covered with boards in which courts were held for several years. It stood about where the South gate of the present court house yard now stands. About the same time a log house was built for a jail, which stood near the South-east corner of the public squqare and near the South-east corner of the drug store lately occupied by Pope and Gordon. A few years after the sale of the lots the Commissioners, from the proceeds of the sale had erected a good brick court house and jail, and also put up stocks as required by the Act of the Legislature. The stocks were put up North of the present court house, near where the North gate of the present yard fence is situated. The sale of the lots was wll attended and they sold for fair prices. A number of houses was soon erected, and the town settled up by enterprising men. Among the first merchants were Richard Scott, David Martin, Jno. Q. Talbot, Jas. Doren, Jno. McCracken and Henry Hagan.

Among the first taverns were Lewis Kirk, on Richland Creek at the foot of the shoals. Captain Thomas (Tubb) Smith on the North-east corner of the square. Alexander, who kept on the South-east corner of the public square at what was known as Kennan's tavern.

Among the first physicians were Dr. Gilbert D. Taylor, Shadrack Nye, David Woods, Alfred Flournoy, Elijah Eldridge, and Charles Perkins, etc.

The first tan yards were established by Jas. Hamby and by Lewis and James Connor; the Connors settled the place where G. W. McGrew's tan yard is at present, and established a yard. Hamby settled the place now owned by Joe B. Childers and established a yard South of his house, near the spring in W. G. Lewis's lot. German Lester was among the first to build a comfortable family residence; he improved the lots now owned by Major B. F. Carter, and lived on them until about 1847. The first resident lawyers were Alfred M. Harris, George Cunningham, Lunsford M. Bramlette, Tryon M. Yancy, W. H. Field, and Aaron V. Brown.

Among the early settlers in the neighborhood of Pulaski not mentioned were David and Wm. Maxwell, Josiah P. Alexander, Wm. W. Woods, Gideon Pillow, the father of General G. J. Pillow, and Captain John Phillips, the father of our present Captain John Phillips. These all settled on Pigeon Roost Creek on the South-west and South. Thomas McKissack, the grandfather of J. T. McKissack, settled the place lately owned by James P. Smith. Thos. Walthall the place on which William D. Abernathy lived, now owned by ———— Short. John Walthall, the place lately owned by Jno. Marks. Thomas Williams, the place on which he long lived on the Lambsferry road. John Williamson, the father of Thos. S. Williamson, in the same neighborhood Hugh Campbell on the place afterwards owned by Captain George Everly and on which he lived until his death.

RESIDENTS OF PULASKI IN 1820

From a copy of the census of Giles County, taken by Charles C. Abernathy in 1820, it appears that the following inhabitants of Pulaski designated as "heads of families" and entered together, and, as it may be interesting to some of their descendants to know that their parents or relatives were here at that date, I will give their names, to-wit: James Perry, Samuel Y. Anderson, Thos. Wilkerson, Jas. Connor, Jno. E. Holden, Wm. English, William Connor, Francis Guthrie, Nathan Alman, William Royle, Bernard M. Patterson, Lunsford M. Bramlette, German Lester, William R. Davis, Robert Gibson, Tryon M. Yancy, Amos David, John Brown, Jesse Day, Francis Hix, William Hamby, Matthias Sharon, Jno. B. Connor, Masterson C. McCormack, Aaron V. Brown, Elizabeth Berry, Judith Burch, Elizabeth Hooks, Mary Scott, William Ball, Thos. White, Joseph H. Hodge, John McCracken, William Rose, Jacob Templin, Peggy Cyrus, Francis Alexander, Joseph Trotter, Robert Crockett, Henry Hagan, Fountain Lester, George Lovell, James Terrill, Archibald Story, Jesse Peebles, Samuel Pearson, Jeremiah Parker, Alf M. Harris, Thomas Smith, William H. Fields, Rebecca Crenshaw, Shadrack Nye, Nathaniel Moody, James Lynch, Alfred Flournoy, James Patterson, Elisha Eldridge, Sallie Collier, John Keenaw, John Hamblett, William Flippen, John Waldrop, Thos. Martin, Charles Perkins.

SECTION FIVE—MORIAH CHURCH, WEAKLEY'S CREEK

Robert Reed, father of Levi Reed, Esquire, settled on the East branch of Weakley's Creek eight miles from Pulaski near where the "Bumpass trail" crossed. He moved from Logan County, Kentucky, came by the Bumpass trail—by Columbia; he built his first cabin on the Chickasaw line and a year or two afterwards had to move it back. John Agnew settled at the mouth of Agnew's Creek for whom it was named. Isaac Lamb, Levi Cooper, John Kitchen and David Campbell settled near the same place and used water from the same spring.

Lawson Hobson settled the place on the East fork of Weakley's Creek, known as the Hobson place; his hands came out with son son Newton a few years before the old man came out They were among the first settlers and came about the time Reed did Some of them may have come before him Valentine Choate settled on Choate's Creek, from whom the creek took its name Major Hurlston settled on Dry Creek, at a very early date and built the first cotton gin that was run by water on Dry Creek where Col. Jas. T.

Wheeler now lives. Owen Sherman and William Wren were among the very first settlers. Wren lived near Robert Reed, Weakley's Creek it is said was named or took its name from Robert Weakley, who was one of the early surveyors. In the Fall of 1809, John Reed the father of Robert Reed came from Kentucky, with eight sons and settled on Weakley's Creek; after he settled on Weakley, and about 1810, Robert Reed and his eight brothers came, of whom was the late Reverend C. P. Reed, and Levi Reed a son of Said Robert Reed all went to school together. The first school taught in the neighborhood was in 1810 by Jno. Morgan. In 1811 a school was taught by the Reverend James B. Porter. Captain James L. Henry was one of the first settlers and was the first constable in his "beat."

Robert Reed and Jonathan Berry were Magistrates in their "beat" (or Captain's Company,) at an early day. Old Reese Porter and his sons, Reese, John, David, Jas. B., and Thos. C. came at an early day and settled near Mount Moriah Church; the old man owned a large tract of land in the neighborhood and settled near what is now Mt. Moriah Church. His sons, David and John settled on the Lawrenceburg road at what has since been called the Connor and Porter places.

The Rev. Jas B., on the Kennedy farm. Thomas C., on the Pullen place at Wales Station; Reese Porter, Jr., died early. He was the father of Reese W. Porter, for many years a merchant and citizen of this County.

There is some discrepancy in dates as to when the Porters came. James L. Henry, who is now in his eighty-seventh year says he came to the neighborhood of Mt. Moriah Church early in 1808 and his recollection is that old Father Porter was there when he arrived. He says he knows that Owen Sherman and Wm. Wren were there also; John Black thinks Sherman and Wren raised corn in the neighborhood in 1806. It is difficult in some cases to reconcile the recollection of old people as to dates; but from the fact that one of the Porter family informs me that he was born in Davidson County in 1808 as he learned from his parents the year or year before they moved to Giles and from other information, I think it probable they came in the latter part of 1808 or early in 1809. In November 1809 the Legislature appointed David Porter one of the first magistrates of the County. He must have been recognized as a resident citizen at that date.

Sampson McCowan and McAllily were early settlers. A man by the name of Gibson first settled on the place where Samuel Gibson now lives, but very soon afterwards was settled by Colonel John Bodenheimer, who lived and died there. He was the father of David Bodenheimer, Esquire, long a magistrate and prominent citizen of our County. Captain Henry says the first marriage in the County that he remembers was Jesse Beaver to Miss Harben, in a little cabin with a dirt floor in the cane-brake, near where Mt. Moriah Church now stands. Says they had bear meat, venison and corn bread for dinner, and hot toddy in tin cups, sweetened with tree sugar. The Cumberland Presbyterian Church at Mt. Moriah was organized in the Fall of 1811. Rev. James B. Porter was the first preacher. Major Hurlston, Thos. Ruby, Reese Porter and Jonathan Berry were the elders. This was the first Cumberland Presbyterian Church organized in the County. In the same Fall a camp meeting was held at that place, and camp ground established.

SEC. SIX—CAMPBELLSVILLE AND BIG CREEK

John Dickey, Esquire, father of James R. Dickey, Esquire, moved from Logan County, Kentucky, and first stopped in Maury and thence to this County in 1808. He cut the cane near the Big Spring at Campbellsville and sowed turnips that Fall, and made a crop of corn in 1809. James Ross, the grandfather of Jas. R. Dickey, came the same Fall and settled the place old Andrew Yokley lived on until his death.

Ross was one of the Commissioners appointed by the Legislature to locate and lay off the town of Pulaski. They traveled the Bumpass trail. The only road at that time coming South from Columbia was the Bumpass trail. They came up Little Bigby, crossed Elk ridge at what is now called the Yokley gap, and came down the Eastern or Yokley branch of Big Creek. The first corn raised in that part of the County was in 1809. Hamilton C. Campbell and Jacob Baylor came about the same time that Dickey did. Jacob Baylor and John Dickey were appointed by the Legislature in November 1809 Magistrates for the "beat" in which they lived. Jas. Ashmore was among the first settlers. He settled the old James Hannah place, one miles North of Campbellsville. He was elected the first constable in his Captain's "beat." Daniel Allen was one of the first settlers and settled at what has since been known as Wright's spring. He erected a powder mill and made powder there for several years. Dan Allen was the father of General Richard H. Allen, for many years a prominent citizen of this County, and afterwards of Lawrence County. John Dickey was elected Representative to the Legislature in 1817. The settlers went to Williamson County the first year for corn. Jacob Bayler built a mill on Dry Creek about one mile West of Campbellsville about 1809 or 1810. This was the first mill built in that part of the country. A mill was built about the same time or soon after on Richland Creek below Moriah Church opposite James Hayes' place, called Mayfield's Mill James R. Dickey was about twelve years old when his father came to the County; says there were but few houses in Columbia when his father moved through there and but few on the road after he left Columbia. Gideon Pillow lived on Little Bigby three miles South of Columbia It was several years after that before he settled the Pillow place in Giles at Wales Station. He says the Bumpass trail came down the Eastern branch of Big Creek, by the old man Ross's and by Mack Alexander's or rather between the two thence South leaving Campbellsville about one mile to the right hand ; it then left Big Creek and took the Dividing Ridge between that creek and Dry Creek, bearing towards Dry Creek and crossing it where Samuel Wilson now lives, and where old Colonel John Bodenheimer lived and died. This trail went rather a zig-zag course to avoid the large cane Cunnigham, who settled the place now owned by John English on the East branch of Big Creek; Jesse Foster, who settled on Dry Creek where Sam Wilson lived; and Kirkland who settled where Jno. I. Morris lived were among the first settlers. Isaac Morris, Sr., and his sons, Matthew Benthal, Peter Swanson, John Wright, Andrew Yokley, Walter Locke, the Gibsons, Reas, Caldwells, Englishes, Alexanders and McCutcheons, Hannahs, Brownlowes, Keltners, Wilcoxes, Shulers, Normans and others, were early settlers; all came before 1820, and some of them among the first; but the dates at which they have not been ascrtained.

SECTION SEVEN—OLD LYNNVILLE AND LYNN CREEK

The first settlers in the Northern part of the County on Lynn Creek and Robertson's Fork crossed Duck River, mostly at Davis's ford, came by where Culleoka now is, and crossed Elk Ridge at Dodson's Gap or went higher up Fountain Creek and crossed farther West. John Fry, father of Captain Wm. Fry moved from the State of North Carolina in the Fall of 1805, crossed the Caney Fork at Stone's River and came by Nashville to Williamson County and stopped on the Harpeth and remained two years and then moved to this County. He came the Davis ford road to Fountain Creek, kept up Fountain Creek by John Richardson's big spring, and crossed Elk Ridge at a gap West of the turnpike gap; went down a branch of the middle prong, and crossed over to the Western prong of Lynn Creek where he settled the eighth of March 1808. William Dearing, George Malone, Gabriel and John Foulkes, and Daniel Harrison settled on the East prong of Lynn Creek in the Fall of 1807. John and Wm. Rutledge, Jacob and Andrew Blythe, Joel Rutledge, and Parrish Simms, settled on the middle prong of Lynn Creek in the Fall of 1807. Nicholas Absolom, and Hugh Barren, Thos. Mooney and Andrew Pickens, settled on the West prong in 1807; most of these raised corn in 1808. John McCabe, John Angus, Jas. Wilsford, Jas. Brownlow and others, settled a little South of John Fry in 1809. John Laird came in December, 1809 and settled the place he lived on for many years on the turnpike half a mile North of Old Lynnville. He crossed Duck River at the Davis Ford, came by John Lindsay's crossed the ridge at the Dodson Gap, came to old Mrs Follis's who lived where Col. T. M. Gordon now lives, and to Lynnville, and from thence to Old Lynnville; he built a mill on the main branch of Lynn Creek, and started the first cotton gin that run by water in that part of the County in 1811. He packed cotton in a square box and pummelled it in with pestles and mauls. He opened a store near his house at an early day and for many years sold goods and without previous training in the business, became a successful merchant. An incident is related illustrative of his character. At a time when he needed an assistant or clerk in

the store he made enquiry of his farmer acquaintances for an
honest respectable, industrious young man of good mind and
good habits. One was suggested, but at the same time he was
told that the young man had been raised on the farm; had
never been from home and knew absolutely nothing of the
mercantile business. He replied that was the kind of a
young man that'he wanted if his other qualities suited; said
he had his own way of doing business and he would rather
undertake to learn a teachable young man who knew nothing
about the business than one whose training differed from his
mode of business. John C. Walker and Elisha White came
about the time Laird did, and settled at Old Lynnville. Walker settled first where White and Walker's store was, and a
year or two afterwards moved East of Elk Ridge Church
where he resided until his death. Elisha White owned the
land on which the town was built and sold out the lots. He
was an energetic and successful man in business. William
Dearing settled the Dearing place one mile North of Old
Lynnville and kept taven on the road. His house was a favorite stopping place for travelers and a noted stage stand for
many years. George Malone first settled by Dearing, but soon
moved to the place one mile South of Old Lynnville on the
turnpike where he lived for many years and died. He was a
successful farmer and one of the first in the County who
raised cotton in considerable quantity for the market. Gabriel
Foulkes first settled where Laird's mill-pond was. Gabriel
and John Foulkes worked in a salt-petre cave, three-fourths
of a mile South-west from Dr. Rutledge's old brick house.
John McCabe settled the Rutledge place about the time Laird
came out. The Tuckers, Wilsfords, Evanses, and English were
early settlers but the dates at which they came have not been
ascertained.

SEC. EIGHT—LYNNVILLE AND LYNNVILLE STATION

John Campbell, Wm. Follis, Nathaniel Moody, John Parch-
ment, Richard and Martin Flint, John Graves, Joel Lane, and
others settled in a colony around what is now Lynnville Station on Robertson's Fork in the Fall of 1809, and raised corn,
the most of them in 1808. Mrs. Follis settled the place on
which Muck Gordon now lives. Nathaniel Moody built the

first mill in the County about half a mile South of Lynnville
on Robertson Fork, near where the railroad crosses it. This
was built in 1808 or early in 1809. The county was established
in November, 1809, and the act establishing the County appointed Nathaniel Moody one of the Commissioners to locate
and lay off the County Seat, to be called Pulaski; he was also
appointed one of the first magistrates of the County. Soon
after the location of the County-seat, he moved to Pulaski and
built a mill on Richland Creek at Pulaski. Hiram and Boyd
Wilson settled the lands over in the valley now owned by
Martin Fry at a very early date, as early as 1809.

SECTION TEN—BUFORD STATION

John Jones, the father of Mrs. Benton R. White and Mrs. A.
A. Dickerson settled the place East of Buford's Station, long
known as the John Jones place; but at present known as the
Fitzpatrick place.

In the early part of 1808, this was for many years a noted
stand on the Davis Ford road from Nashville to Pulaski and
considerable business was done at it in the early days. Andrew M Ballentine opened a store there in 1815, and sold
goods there for a number of years before he moved to Pulaski
At the same time John Jones settled the place aforesaid, Samuel Jones, his brother, settled at a place about a mile East,
now owned by Mrs. Judge Spofford. John White settled near
where Buford Station is, and built a mill on Robertson's
Fork, just above the Station. Ostin Carter and John Pate settled on lands now owned by A. A. Dickerson. Robert Guthrie
and Colonel L. Cleaveland of King's Mountain memory, came
about the time John and Sam Jones came, or soon after. They
all raised corn in 1808. Col. Cleaveland settled on part of the
farm now owned by Mrs. Judge Spofford where he died; and
his grave is near the building occupied by the Superintendent
of the farm. John Jones died in 1823, and Sam Jones in 1815.
He was killed by a tree falling on him. About the time John
Jones came or soon afterwards, David and Alexander Jones
settled in the same neighborhood. Rebecca Jones, widow of
David Jones, is still living and is over ninety years of age. Col
Robert Steele, brother of Thos. and David Steele settled on
the West side of the creek opposite Buford Station, about the

time the Joneses came. He was Colonel of the first regiment organized in the County. William and Henry Sheppard settled the place on which Albert Buford lived at an early date. Richard, Matthew and John Johnson and Jack Miller settled the places long known by their names on Haywood Creek at a very early day. James Tinnon the father of Robert and Aleck Tinnon, and Joseph and David Abernathy, were early settlers on Richland and Haywood in the neighborhood of Tinnon's Mill.

The settlers on Haywood came some of them in 1808, others about 1809 or 1810. Tinnon and the Abernathys it is said, came by the Bumpass trail, leaving it somewhere South of Campbellsville.

I regret that I have not the information to give a more extended notice of Col. Cleaveland, one of the immortal heroes of King's Mountain. Judge Spofford has kindly furnished the following transcription from the inscription on his tomb:

"SACRED"

To the Memory of Col. Larkin Cleaveland
Formerly of Franklin County, Georgia.
Born April 1748. Died July 9, 1814.

SECTION TEN—ELK RIDGE CHURCH

John Montgomery and Sam Montgomery settled on Robert son's Fork near Elk Ridge Church early in 1808, and crossed the ridge at what was first called the Sam Montgomery gap, and afterwards known as the Dodson Gap. Leander M. Shields, father of John M. Shields, came in 1809 and settled near the church where he lived many years. Samuel Shields and James Shields came about the same time or soon after and settled in the same neighborhood. Samuel Shields was the father of the Honorable Ebenezer J .Shields—for several years a Representative in Congress from that district, and one of the most graceful and elegant public speakers our County has produced Joseph Braden, the grandfather of Major J. B. Stacy, Achibald Crockett, Alexander Shields, Robert Crockett, Samuel Copeland and James Montgomery were early settlers. John C. Walker, after remaining a short time at Old Lynnville settled on the road East of the Church where he lived for many years and until his death. East of Walker's, and in the same neighborhood were Presley and Robert Topp; William James, William Ussery, and Hugh Caruthers, Samuel Patrick, Ephraim Patrick, Ephraim M. Massey and William Marr. These were all early settlers; some of them among the very first but the dates at which they came have not been ascertained with sufficient certainty to give them.

SECTION ELEVEN

Brick Church and Robert Gordon Neighborhood

Robert Gordon with his sons, Thos. K. and John, settled on Richland Creek near the Brick Church at what was long known as the Gordon place—the third of March 1808, and made a crop that year; cultivated 11 acres in corn; he moved from Kentucky ten miles from Crab Orchard to Williamson County, Tennessee, and settled nine miles West of Franklin and two miles from Gideon where he lived two years and then removed to Giles. He was in the outside settlement when he lived in Williamson. In coming to this County he traveled the old McCutcheon trail. It passed East of Spring Hill, crossed Duck River at what was afterwards known as Holland's Ferry above Davis's Ford; passed by the widow McNutt's not far from where Mooresville is situated. The old trace passed a little West of where he settled; went by the old Brick Church thence South to Elk River at Shoemaker's Ferry near Latitude Hill. From McNutt's to where Gordon settled was twelve milees and McNutt's was the last house he passed; and there were but few settlers between McNutt's and where he moved from in Williamson County. Two or three families were in the neighborhood before Gordon came. A man named Vaughan was living at the spring on the widow Mary Gordon's place, half a mile North of where Robert Gordon, Sr., settled. The widow Clark and two or three of her sons had settled on the Marsh and Wood farms.

There were no settlers for six miles in a North-east direction to Jno. Henderson and James S. Haynes; they came about the same time Gordon did, and settled the places long known by their names near Cornersville. Going West down Richland Creek there were not any settlers nearer than John or Sam Jones' and they were six miles off. In a Southern direction, it was ten miles to Robert Alsup's who lived on the

South-west side of Pisgah Hill. Soon after Gordon came, Joseph Jarmin and old John McCandless and his sons and their families came. A man named Nation, with several sons, settled the Robert H. Laird place South of the old Brick Church. For the first two years they packed the most of their meal on horses from Williamson County. The first year some of the settlers used hand mills. Martin Lane, Sr., and his son-in-law. Thos. Lane, Esquire, came about two years after Gordon. The Fraziers, Tungetts and Samuels came about the time Lane did. Gordon's oldest daughter, Elizabeth, was married the first of February, 1810 to Joseph McDonald, two weeks before the courts were organized in Giles and they went to Maury County for license and were married at the widow McNutt's by John Lindsay, Esquire. The father of William and David Maxwell owned the land on Pigeon Roost settled by them and sent out a man named Milroy with his stock to improve it. This was before Gordon came and a year or two afterwards Wm. and David came out to live on the land. Richard McGehee lived one and a half miles West of Gordon; was an early settler and one of the first magistrates in that part of the County. John Dabney, Sr., settled about one mile North of Gordon at a very early day. James S. Haynes and his father, John Haynes, old William Henderson, and his brother, John Henderson, and Jno. Andrews were among the first settlers in the neighborhood of Cornersville and came about the time Gordon did. At that time there was a trace from Cornersville that intersected the McCutcheon trail South of Gordon, near where the old Brick Church stood. The cane had been chopped so that people could ride along it. This trace and the old McCutcheon trace were the only roads opened when Gordon came.

SECTION TWELVE—BRADSHAW

Odem Hightower, father of Hardy Hightower, was one of the first settlers on Bradshaw Creek, and came either the latter part of 1807 or early in 1808. He raised corn in 1808, which was the first raised on the creek.

Hardy Hightower, John Kennedy, John Elliff, James McKnight, and Sam McKnight came the latter part of 1808, or early in 1809, and settled the placees known by their names. Joe Jarmin came in the early part of 1808, John Young, Esquire, was one of the first settlers. John Young settled the place known as the Archibald Young place. Nicholas Holly, father of Jno. Holly, came in February or March 1809.

Those mentioned above were all here when Holly came. The first year the settlers beat most of their meal in a mortar and ground some in a little hand-mill. Hardy Hightower built the first mill on Bradshaw. Old Nicholas Holly moved from South Carolina to the State of Ohio, and from thence to Tennessee. He came by Columbia, by where Jno. C. Walker, Esquire, lives; by Dabney's and by old Robert Gordono's.

SECTION THIRTEEN—MT. PISGAH

The first settlement about Mount Pisgah was by the Reverend Alex MacDonald and his brothers, Joseph, Robert and John; and his relatives Major William MacDonald and James MacDonald, all of whom came in the latter part of 1808. MacDonald settled the place now owned by Sterling Abernathy. John MacDonald, where Col. Willis Worley now lives. Maj. William MacDonald where William Oliver now lives. Joseph Alsup came before the MacDonalds about the first of 1808, and settled in the hollow over the hill South of Alex MacDonald's. The old man Maples and his sons came about the time or before the MacDonalds, and lived in the hollow above MacDonald's. Laban Westmoreland, the grandfather of Dr. Theo. Westmoreland settled near the John Neal place West of Mt. Pisgah hill. He came to the County about the time his brothers, Jesse and Thomas came in the latter part of 1808 or early in 1809.

He raised a crop in 1809, although his family might not have come until the latter part of the year. Aquilla Wilson, the Stovalls, Tilman R. Daniel, George Oliver, the Bradleys, Rickman Williams and Craft were early settlers in the neighborhood but the dates have not been ascertained. The first camp meeting at Mt. Pisgah was in 1811 and held near where William Oliver lived about half a mile North of Mt. Pisgah Church. In 1812 the camp meeting was held at Mount Pisgah and kept up for many years.

SECTION FOURTEEN

Blooming Grove Church and Leatherwood Creek

Thomas Marks, father of Edward and Maj. Lewis B.

Marks came to the County the first of January, 1811, and settled the place Jacob Reasonover lives on. James Dugger, Esquire, came at the same time, and settled on the place Carroll Marks now lives. They came from Davidson County by Columbia, crossed Richland Creek at John Jones's, now Fitzpatrick's; came the Gideon road to Pulaski; camped the first night at William Gideon's, near the factory, and thence traveled over Locust Hill to Leatherwood Creek; kept on the ridge because the cane was small on the ridge, and there was no undergrowth of timber or bushes, and in some places no cane Where there was no cane the ground was covered with peavines. They kept along the ridge and went down at the point where William Arrowsmith lived; and when they struck the creek they kept up the bed of the creek to avoid the large cane, and even cut a log that was across the creek and rolled it out to travel the bed of the creek as far as they could, in preference to cutting their way through the large cane on the creek bottoms. Maj. Nathan Davis settled the Daniel Abernathy place and Capt. Thos. C. Stone, the place now owned by John M. White at a very early day; as early probably as 1808 or 1809. They settled a year or two before Marks came. A man named Stevens lived where Edward Marks now lives in January 1811. Old Tom Webb lived West of the creek on the top of the hill on the place owned by Arrowsmith heirs. Thos. McKerly built a house near where Mrs. Arrowsmith lives.

Old man Patite first settled on Locust Hill, where old Silas Flournoy settled. Flournoy came about 1813. Shade Harwell and Henry Loyd moved to the County the winter that Thos. Marks came. Austin Smith settled the place East of the Creek that Doll Hopkins lives at. Allen Abernathy was one of the first settlers in the neighborhood as was Austin Smith. At the time Thomas Marks came to the County about the last of December, 1810, or the first day of January, 1811, his son Edward was ten years old and Lewis B., eight years old.

SECTION FIFTEEN—BUNKER HILL AND INDIAN CREEK

Benjamin Benson, Earley Benson, Valentine Huff, William Watson, Isham Brown and his son; old Wm. Birdwell and his son, John Birdwell, Jesse Lamb, Adam Bell and John Lamb were very early settlers on Indian Creek, and around

Bunker Hill and the most of them, if not all of them, came the latter part of 1808 or the first of 1809, and made corn in 1809. Adam Bell came the McCutcheon trace. The Birdwells settled on what has long been known as the Robert McLaurine place. John Lamb settled the place where Thomas P. Brooks now lives; he and his son moved from there to Lamb's Ferry on the Tennessee River. They established the ferry and from them it took its name. Isaac Lamb settled on the Northeast corner of the Jno. Bass field, where the old graveyard is. Dr. Silas McGuire settled on the Joe Rowe place. Thomas Stanford, Sr., came in the latter part of 1808 or in 1809, and settled on the West side of Indian Creek at the ford where old Mrs. Jolly afterwards lived. James Redus. Caleb Freily, William McGuire and John Manarke came in 1809 or 1810, and settled on the place afterwards called the Jno. McCormack place, or near there. Drury Alsup, in the early part of 1809 settled the place on which Nathan Bass lived; and made corn in 1809. Duncan Bown, and Daniel McCallum moved from Sumner County in the Fall of 1809; came by Columbia and by way of the Bumpass trail to Crosswater where they remained a week or two, and settled about six miles South-east of Crosswater, at the place now owned by Henry Watson. For two-thirds of the way after they left Crosswater they cut the cane to open a road for their wagons and this trail furnished a branch road for others to travel going in that dircetion. They arrived at the place they settled the 10th day of December, 1809. In 1810 or 1811, Captain John Smith from Glasgow, Scotland, settled near Duncan Brown's. He had been a sailor for many years; was in the British Navy, and was with Nelson in the great Naval battle of Trafalgar. About 1811 or 1812, Aqulla Wilson settled near McCallum on the North and Matthew Murcrief, Sr., on the South. A few years later James Paine, Esq., father of Bishop Paine, settled the Paine place one mile North-east from where McCallum lived and about the same time Robert Paine, Edward Shelton, Larkin Cardin, and Wm. B. Brooks, settled about a mile South of where Brown settled. Among the first settlers on Indian Creek not named were Larkin Webb, John Reasonover, Kinchew Bass, North of Bunker Hill; and John and Richard Wright, and old Jesse Perry and his sons; Buckner, Madry, William Sawyers,

John Sanford, Henry and John Naive, and Daniel Molloy South of it. A few years later Willis S. McLaurine, Robert McLaurine, Wm. McLaurine, Thos. Wells, Arnold Zealnor, Josiah Phelps, John McCormack, and Martin Baugh, settled in the neighborhood. Indian Creek Church, Primitive Baptist was organized in 1811. George Brown was the first preacher, and in 1811 Mrs. Nathan Bass, and Mrs. William Watson were baptized and joined the Church. It is believed they were the first cases of baptism in that Church. Samuel McKnight, Wm. B. Brooks and Anold Zealnor were prominent members.

SECTION SIXTEEN—ELKTON AND NEIGHBORHOOD

The first settlements in the County were on Elk River, about the mouth of Richland Creek. At an early day a road or way of travel was opened on the West side of the creek from the "Bumpass trail," through the settlements to the mouth of Richland. A similar road was also opened on the East side, from Crosswater to the mouth of the creek long known as the lower Elkton road. Soon after the County was organized John and Wm. Price laid off a town and sold out lots at the mouth of the creek and the place was called Lower Elkton. It became an important shipping point and considerable business was done at it for fifteen or twenty years. Soon after a town was established at the mouth of the creek, Dr. Burnell and others laid off a town on the river, three miles above and sold out lots, etc., at what is now Elkton proper; and to distinguish them, one was called Lower Elkton and one Upper Elkton. After the shipping of produce by flat boats was abandoned, Lower Elkton went down, and the distinction of Upper and Lower Elkton ceased. The neighborhood of Elkton was settled two or three years before the town was laid off.

William Phillips came in the Fall of 1808 and settled the Phillips place two miles North of Elkton. He moved from Davidson County and traveled the McCutcheon trace. William Menefee, Sr., and his sons, John and William, and his son-in-law, Benjamin Long, were among the first settlers. They came from Lincoln County, Kentucky; traveled what was called the Kentucky trace; came over the Cumberland Mountains, crossed Elk River near the head of it; came along the State Line and the old man Menefee stopped on the South side of the river opposite Elkton and settled above the ferry where Samuel Fain afterwards put up a distillery. This was about the middle of November, 1808. The old man died the following March. John Menefee settled soon afterward on the Huntsville road three miles South-east of Elkton where William S. Ezell now lives. William Menefee Jr., settled one mile North of his brother John. Benjamin Long settled half a mile North of Elkton where Dick Baugh lives at the Big Spring, near where Hanserd lives. No person then lived in Elkton. Benjamin Long was the first to settle near the town. Mrs. Lucinda Laughlin, who is a daughter of William Menefee, Sr., and a sister of Benjamin Long's wife says she was nearly twenty years of age when her father came; that there was not a "cane amiss" where Elkton is situated. She says, at the time her father came, John Shoemaker was living at the ferry on the river above Elkton called Shoemaker's ferry near where the old McCutcheon trace crossed the river. She was married the eighth of March, 1810, to Alexander Laughlin by Wm. Phillips, Esquire. The license was the first issued by German Lester, Clerk of the County Court, etc., and is now in the possession of Captain George Bowers. She was twenty-one years old when she married Alexander Laughlin; then lived on the South side of the river at Shoemaker's ferry, and was here a year before her father came. He kept salt and flour to sell. He came from East Tennessee, came down the Holston in a boat and brought salt and flour. He and two of the Massengales, brothers of his first wife, owned a boat; they lived on the Holston and boated down salt, flour, and other commodities and Laughlin sold for them. Of the first settlers now living (1876), Mrs. Laughlin was older when she came than any I have conversed with in the last year. I have conversed with none who has a more vivid and distinct recollection than she has of early times. She states that at the time her father moved to this County, her brothers Renlar and Laban were boys living with her father, and her brother Jarrett Menefee came out the next Fall. William Phillips and Benjamin Long were appointed Justices of the Peace in 1809. They were the first Magistrates in the Southern part of the County. Captain Thos. Phillips built the first house in what is now the town of Ekton the latter part of 1810.

Captain John Hawkins, Dr. William Purnell, Captain James Perrill, Thos. Harwood, and Gustin Kerney came at an early day, about the latter part of 1810, or the first part of 1811. Kerney came a year or so later than the others. These with Thos. Phillips were among the first settlers in Elkton. Wm. and Jno. Price, Alex and John Baldridge settled near the mouth of Richland Creek on the East side at an early day; probably about the latter part of 1808, and settled what was afterwards Lower Elkton.

William Sawyers, Buckner Madry, and John Sanford settled the place Ben Osborne now lives on, called the Shelton place, about the latter part of 1808 or first of 1809; and after living there a year or two settled in the hollow West or South-west of the Birdwell place. After they left the place was purchased by James Bumpass and his son-in-law, Maxmillian H. Buchanan, (the grandfather) and the father of Mrs. Solon E. Rose. They lived on the place several years and sold to Edmund Shelton. He lived on it for many years. Old man Perry and his sons ,Jno., Wm., Alex, and George, and one or two younger ones settled the place afterwards owned by Duncan Brown on which he lived for many years and until his death. On this place, Ex-Governors Neill S., and John C. Brown were raised, and on which the latter was born. The former was born on the place his father first settled about two miles North-west. In the latter part of 1814, Daniel McCallum moved from the place he first settled about two miles south and settled the place on which he lived for many years, and until his death in 1830, being half a mile West of Duncan Brown, one mile East of James Bumpass, and four miles North of Elkton. In 1808 and 1809 Brice M. Garner brought a boatload of salt down the Tennessee River and up Elk as far as Shoemaker's ferry, with a vew of carrying it to Fayetteville, but the stage of the water was such that he could not get his boat over the shoal above the ferry; and he stopped there and built a house near the ferry in twenty yards of the river, stored his salt and sold it out The place was called the salt house for a long time. Salt was brought up the river in keel boats and sold there for several years. In 1811, John McCracken sold goods at the salt house, being on the old McCutcheon trace. It was a noted stand and place for crossing the river.

For the first three years the principal travel from Pulaski and the places North of it to Huntsville crossed at Shoemaker's. From Pulaski the first road went out by MacDonald's and over the ridge by where John Neil now lives to the McCutcheon trace; down Indian Creek by John Birdwell and John Lamb's to Shoemaker's. Irishtown on Silver Creek, embracing the Sotuhern part of the land lated owned by Wm. L. Brown, on the turnpike was settled March, 1810 by Hugh Campbell. Four men by the name of Phillips (all Irish), a man named White and one by the name of Snipes, and others; Joab Campbell came a year or two later.

In the Fall of 1816, at a muster at William Phillips' the great fight between the Prices and McKinneys came off. James Price and James McKinney were the principals. Joab Campbell was the friend of the Prices, and Phelps and Jno. Smith of the McKinneys. There was no special quarrel between the principals. The Prices were regarded as "champions" in their neighborhood and the McKinneys in theirs. One of the principals asked the other which of his family was regarded as the best man He replied that he thought he was. The other told him to prepare himself for a fight. They engaged. They were both champions in size, physical development, game, and endurance. It was a most desperate fight and continued long. Their friends became engaged and at one time a half dozen fights were going on. The crowd became excited and almost half of them stripped to fight, without having any particular person in view to fight, or anything in particular to fight about. To one who never witnessed such a scene the effect is indescribable. The writer was then a boy. It was the first fight he ever saw and was the most gigantic one he has ever seen. Price and his friends were victorious.

Samuel Woods settled the Goode place now owned by James M. King in 1812. Previous to that George Stanford lived there, and made the first improvment. John Manaske lived on the place afterward known as the Jno. McCormack place and made powder there on a small scale. Colonel James Terrell settled the place where Dr. James A .Bowers now lives. Colonel Gustin Kerney settled the place where old Jacob Miller first lived when he came to Elkmont a few hundred yards South of Dr. Bower's residence. The road from Elkton to Pulaski was cut out in the Fall of 1810 or Spring of 1811. Wm. Phillips was overseer of the hands to open it from Elkton to Paine's Hill; about half the distance. Mrs. Laughlin says, that after her marriage in March, 1810, to Alex Laughlin they lived on the Duty place, South of the river at Shoemaker's ferry; and while living there the earth-quakes occurred. She says Nicholas and Sam Fain had the first stores in Elkton. That Talbot, a lame man, clerked for them, or was in the store with them; that some time after they came, Taylor and Mc-Ewin had a store there, and Maj. John Bass was in partnership with them. The Fains and Bass were merchants in Elkton for many years. They were men of the highest integrity, popular and successful in business.

SECTION SEVENTEEN—SHOAL AND SUGAR CREEKS

It will be remembered that by the treaty of 1805, the Chickasaw Indians parted with their right to the land, North and East of a line run from the South-west corner of Maury County to Ditto's landing on the Tennessee River; and that all the land South and West of that line remained Indian territory until the treaty of September, 1816. Consequently the South-western part of the County could not be settled as early as the Northern and Eastern parts, although a considerable portion of the land had been entered before 1790.

The first settlers were Reuben Riggs and Henry Morgan. They lived on the place afterwards owned by Carey Gilbert. William Noblitt, James McKinney and Kallit Nail were very early settlers. Nail lived at the Black place or at the foot of what was called Nail's Hill, now called Minor Hill. James Collins was also one of the first settlers. All these were living on Indian territory at the time the United States soldiers drove the settlers back and destroyed their crops and improvements. Many of them were driven off and their crops and improvements destroyed. After the treaty of Stptember, 1816 the lands on the Indian side of the line were mostly secured or purchased by the settlers and that portion of the County was rapidly settled up. James Paisley in 1818, settled the old Paisley place, and in 1820 built a horse mill.

Elijah Anthony settled there in 1817, and erected a water mill at what is called Shores' Mill. In 1818, Mrs. Mary E. Gooch, mother of Daniel A. Gooch, Esq., settled on Shoal Creek, at the Gooch place; and about the same time Captain Jerry Barnes, Hezekiah Jones and David Jonees, James White, Esq., settled in the neighborhood.

Mrs. Gooch made a crop in 1818. In the same year four families of the Brownings, Mat Davenport, Sam and John Hopper, James Hammonds, Asa McGee, John Boyd and Nathan Carroll, settled in the neighborhood. Reuben Riggs raised corn on the Gilbert place, and Collins on the Daniel Jones place at an early date; they are believed to be the first or among the first who raised corn in the neighborhood.

The first Church organized was by the Cumberland Presbyterians in 1818, at Paisley's. Reverend Robert Donald and Reverend A. Smith were the preachers.

Sugar Crek was settled in 1818 by Samuel Cox, Jesse Marlow, and his sons; the Appletons, Tuckers, Glen and others. These named were among the first settlers. Cox built a mill at the place known as Malone's Mill. There was an Indian trail leading from Nail's Hill (now Minor Hill), towards Huntsville and perhaps to Huntsville. It was two or three feet wide; some of the first settlers claim to have driven hogs along this trail.

CHAPTER V

ORIGIN OF LAND TITLES AND LAND WARRANTS

To explain to the rising generation the origin of our land titles, and the reason why so many of our first settlers lost their lands by conflict of title, it is necessary to briefly recur to the legislation of North Carolina, in relation to her Western territory and the mode adopted for the payment of her soldiers and the public debt; together with the action of Congress in relation thereto.

To carry on the war of the Revolution, the Provincial Congress had neither money nor credit, and the State of North Carolina issued scrip to pay her soldiers and the expenses of the war, and made it a legal tender. The scrip depreciated until at the close of the war it was almost worthless. With the feelings of a mother for her unfortunate children, the State resolved to make up to her soldiers all they had lost by the depreciation of her scrip, and adopted a scale of depreciation for every month in the year, from 1777 to 1782, and provided for the auditing of all accounts for such depreciation; and issued her certificates for the specie value thereof which she provided might be exchanged for land warrants at fifty cents per acre; and opened a land office at Hillsboro, N. C., called John Armstrong's office, for the sale of Western land and the entry of all warrants issued in payment of the public debt, and as a permanent reward for the patriotism and zeal of her soldiers, gave lands to them; to each private six hundred and forty acres, and advancing with the officers according to grade, and appropriated a tract of country on the North side of Middle Tennessee fifty-five miles wide. Commencing where the Virginia line crossed the Cumberland River, and West to the Tennessee River, and issued Warrants for the same,—called Military Warrants, and established an office in Nashville, calling it Martin Armstrong's office, for the entry of the same, giving the preference to the officers and soldiers within the district thus appropriated. In 1782 the General Assembly appointed Absolum Tatum, Isaac Shelby and Anthony Bledsoe, Commissioners to lay off the lands appropriated to the officers and soldiers; and also twenty-five thousand acres donated to General Greene, and provided that the Governor should appoint a suitable guard, with the requisite officers, not to exceed one hundred men to accompany the Commissioners. Early in 1783 the Commissioners, with a guard and a large number of the settlers, on the Cumberland, set out from Nashville to Harpeth Glades on the Big South Road, and traveled South across the State, crossing Duck River near the mouth of Flat Creek, at what was called the Shallow Ford, and crossing Robertson's Fork and Richland, and down Bradshaw to within one or one and a half miles of the mouth, where it rained so as to raise Elk River past fording; they then went down the river to where the McCutcheon trace crossed it, and then on a high bluff on the North side of the river took their astronomical observations, to ascertain the thirty-fifth degree of North latitude. Gen. Daniel Smith took the observation, and by his calculation they were about three miles from the South boundary of the State. The river being past fording their purpose was to make a canoe, and send over some of the party to go to the South boundary, but finding a good deal of Indian signs and Indian horses, they finally concluded not to cross. They marked a number of trees on the hill with the names of those present, and the date, and turned back. The place has since been called "Latitude Hill." Among the settlers who accompanied the Commissioners were the Bledsoes, Shelbys, Casselmans, McCutcheons, Bradshaws, Elijah Robertson, General Jams Robertson, General Dan. Smith and others, being sixty or eighty in all some of them doubtless going as part of the guard allowed.

These were the first white men that explored Giles County, or were ever through it so far as is now known. They gave names to most of the creeks, and located or took notes for locating a considerable portion of the best lands in the County. Gen. James Robertson named Richland. Elijah Robertson Robertsons Fork and Haywood; Bradshaw and Indian Creeks were named at that time but it is not known by whom. After they left "Latitude Hill" they went up Indian Creek and over to the head of Buchanan Creek, and thence to Haywood where they camped the first night. After they left Elk River Elijah Robertson located a tract of five thousand acres for John Haywood and it is believed named the Creek; from Haywood they went over to Fountain Creek, and after going down Fountain Creek to the fork, went down Duck River to the Bigby, and below Columbia laid off twenty-five thousand acres for General Greene. The Commissioners estimating the State to be one hundred and ten miles wide at a point fifty-five miles North from the Southern boundary as ascertained by them, run a line West to the Tennessee River; East as far as where the Cumberland River crossed the North boundary of the State, assigning all North of that line as the district st apart for the officers and soldiers. The next Assembly which met the same year, at the request of the officers directed it to be laid off; from the North boundary running fifty-five miles South which was run accordingly in the Spring of 1784 by General Rutherford.

The laast line is eight or nine miles farther South than the first one. In 1783, after the close of the war the General Assembly of North Carolina, declared her boundary to begin at the lines which separates that State from the State of Virginia; thence with that line West to the Mississippi river thence; down the river to the thirty-fifth degree of North Latitude; and East to the Appalachian mountains; and after assigning new boundaries to the Cherokee Indians in East Tennessee, appropriated all other vacant lands in the State whether claimed by Cherokees or Chickasaws to the redemption of her public debt, and to satisfy the claims of her officers and soldiers; and opened offices for entering the same.

The treaty of peace having been signed in' Paris in November 1782, although not fully ratified until Feb. 1, 1783; and the whole State being open to location and entry; and every holder of the warrants permitted to enter wherever he chose, saving the lands in East Tennessee assigned to the Cherokee Indians and the district reserved for the officers and soldiers. Very soon a host of warrant-holders, locators and surveyors, traversed the State from the mountains to the Mississipp River making locations for which no system had been adopted; no road or path led from one part of the State to another except a few Indian trails. The creeks and streams were unknown and without name. These were named by the first exporers and sometimes different names were given to the same stream.

To add to their difficulties the Indians were greatly exasperated at the entering of their lands, so that much of the land so located was done by stealth, as it were, for fear of the Indians. Having no concert of action two or three locations were occasionally made on the same land, and often the calls of one entry conflicted with those of another. The description of land located was often indefinite; so much so that many of them could not afterwards be identified. As an illustration: One location in the South-east part of the County described the land as beginning on a particular "tree, on the bank of the branch where we camped the night and killed the bear." While these men lived the land could probably be identified but not by strangers. After the organization of the Federal Government, the States having within their boundaries unappropriated land were urged to cede them to the General Government as a common fund for the payment of the public debt. None of the States except Virginia, Georgia, and North Carolina, had any unappropriated land within their boundary. Virginia claimed all that immense territory out of which has been made the States of Kentucky, Illinois, Indiana, Michigan and Wisconsin; and with a liberality worthy the "Mother of Statesmen" ceded all her unappropriated country North of the Ohio River reserving only a small portion for the satisfaction of her military warrants. The residents in what is now Kentucky, had already taken steps to become an independent State. Georgia claimed all the territory West of the Chattahoochie, to the Mississippi, between the parallels of 31 and 35 degrees of North Latitude out of which the States of Alabama and Mississippi have been formed. She refused to cede her territory, or to recognize the right of the Federal government to interfere therewith and made two efforts to sell her territory to certain Companies called the "Zazoo Companies" one of which was the Tennessee Zazoo Company composed of Zachariah Cox and others, embracing a number of the most prominent men in Tennessee who, in 1795, purchased all North Alabama for sixty-five thousand dollars; and attempted to sell it. But those sales were opposed by the Federal Government and all attempts to sell the territory under these purchases called the Zazoo purchas was prohibited. Georgia finally repealed the Act and ceded to the United States her territory in 1802 for one million, two hundred and fifty thousand dollars. The object of Georgia was by enlisting individual enterprise, to have her territory speedily settled, and thus protect her citizens against the Indians.

North Carolina, by Act of General Assembly, in December, 1789, ceded her territory West of what is now her West boundary to the General Government subject to the satisfaction of all her land warrants and the fullfillment of all her just obligations to her own citizens.

The deed of cession was signed in 1790, and soon after accepted. In the same year the Federal Government organized the territory thus ceded into a territorial government calld the territory of the United States South of the Ohio, and appointed Wm. Blount, Governor. Soon after the cession the Federal Government by Act of Congress, stopped the entering of land in the territory ceded and declared all entries made after the cession void.

In June, 1796, Tennessee was admitted into the Union as a State and on her admission a Bill was introduced in Congress enacting a forfeiture of all rights to lands in Indian territory, in case the claimants should go on the land or have it surveyed or the lines marked. Some of the delegates from States that had no land to cede were dissatisfied at the small amount likely to be realized from the public land in Tennessee; and took the ground that entries made on lands to which the Indian title had not been extinguished, were void; that the State of North Carolina could convey no title, having no title herself. This gave rise to a debate on the subject of the tenure of the Indians in which Mr. Madison, Mr. Gallatin, and others, took part. Mr. Madison said, "It was unnecessary to investigate the Indian mode of occupancy, and opposition to civilized society; that all the Nations in Europe who had possessed territories on the American Continent held that the Indians had only a qualified property in the soil; that if it was conceded that they have an unqualified title, they could not be prevented from ceding to foreign governments their lands within the limits of the United States."

Mr. Gallatin took the same view, and both sustained the

right of North Carolina to dispose of her lands as she had done.

CHAPTER VI—CONGRESSIONAL RESERVATION

By the terms of the cession of 1790, the Federal Government was bound to fulfill in good faith all the obligations of the State of North Carolina to her citizens at that time, thousands of warrants had not been located or extended, and no office having been opened for the entry of the same the State of Tennessee became impatient at such delay, and through her Legislature in 1801 claimed the right to dispose of all the vacant and unappropriated land within her boundaries, and appointed her Senators and Representatives in Congress her agents to have her claims settled. The result was a compromise; and to carry out said settlement Congress passed an Act in April 1806 requiring a line to be run beginning where Elk River intersects the Southern boundary of the State of Tennessee, thence North to Duck, thence down Duck, to the line of the district reserved for the officers and soldiers of the Continental line; thence with said boundary to the Tennessee River; thence down the river to the North boundary of the State, and upon the State of Tennessee relinquishing all claims to the lands South and West of this line, the United states ceded to the state of Tennessee all the claims to the land North and East of said line; subject to the conditions of the original act of cession of North Carolina and for the purpose therein prescribed; and subject to the express condition that all entries of land, rights of location, warrants of survey, etc., not actually located North and East of said line and subject to the further condition that the State of Tennessee shall appropriate one hundred thousand acres of land in one body—in the lands reserved for the Cherokee Indians in East Tennessee for the use of two colleges, one in East Tennessee, and the other in West Tennessee and one hundred thousand acres in one tract within the limits thus ceded for the use of County Acadamies, one to be established in each County, and six hundred and forty acres of land in every six miles where existing claims will permit for the use of schools for the instruction of children. To ascertain the Southern boundary of the State, with reference to running the line contemplated by the Act of Congress a party of surveyors went out in 1806. I have been unable to find any report or record of their proceedings, although I have had search made in the archives of this State; and of the State of North Carolina, and also the General land office at Washington. They doubtless made rpeort, as the Legislature declined to adopt the line run by them. James Bright was one of the surveyors The line was called Bright's line; it passed through the land I first lived on. My deeds call for it. From my youth I had heard the tradition of the country in relation to it; I heard James Bright on several occasions talk about it, but I have no recollection that he stated where they took their observations. Two places have been assigned to the traditions of the country—one at Latitude Hill in Giles County and the other farther East in Lincoln County. From my early impressions I believe it was Latitude Hill and and so stated several years ago over my signature, which was published. From a recent investigation I am now of opinion that the observations were taken in Lincoln County, but whatever discrepancy there may be as to the place at which the ogservations were taken they all substantially agree that the surveyors, not having full confidence, either in their instruments or in the accuracy of their observations, were influenced to some extent by the observations taken at Latitude Hill by the Commissioners in 1873 and probably by measurement, and stopped a little short of their own calculations, and from the point thus ascertained, run West, striking Elk River at the head of the island above the Freeman mill about a mile below Elkton, and from the West bank the river run North at a variation of six and a half degrees, West for the true meridian, passing West of Elkton, and crossing the turnpike road about a mile North of Elkton and striking Duck River about eight miles above Columbia. This line was called the Old Congressional Reservation line or Bright's Line.

In September, 1806, the Legislature, being dissatisfied with the line as run, appointed Gen. John Strother a Commissioner on the part of the State to ascertain the point at which the Southern boundary of the State crossed Elk River etc.

They provided that he should be attended by the surveyor of the Second District (William P. Anderson,) and requested the Governor to communicate with the proper authorities at Washington and request the co-operation of the United

States Government.

In October, 1807, General Strother and Wm. P. Anderson, on the part of the State of Tennessee, and Col. Meigs, as is believed, on the part of the United States government, with Thos. Freeman as mathematician commenced at a point twenty miles East of Elk River in Lincoln County. On the time adopted by the surveyors the years before and probably at the same place, and there the observations were taken by Freeman on the twelfth, fourteenth, and fifteenth of October 1807, for the determination of the South boundary of the State or the 35 degree of North Latitude which they ascertained to be two-miles 242.58 poles South of the place of observation, being about two and three-fourths miles further South than the temporary line adopted by the surveyors the year before. From the point thus ascertained, they run West striking Elk River at the mouth of Jenkins Creek and from the right or West bank of the River run North at variation of six and a half degrees West from the true meridian; passing two and one-fourth miles West of Prospect, passing the East margin of Pulaski and striking Duck River near the Eastern margin of Columbia a short distance above the bridge, and thence down the river. And here I beg leave to relate an incident that occurred while Strother's line was being run, told to me by James Bright of Fayetteville. He was then a young man and engaged as a surveyor by Wm. P. Anderson, and Judge McNairy of Nashville who was largely interested in locating and entering land. By agreement with Anderson Bright was to meet him on the lines before they reached Duck River. Bright wnt to Columbia on his way to meet him. There was then only two or three houses where Columbia is situated. A man named Estes lived there; he traveled from thence South by his compass through the woods and came to no house on his way, until he came near to where Campbell Station is. There he found a family in a log cabin recently put up at which he stopped—but the occupants had nothing for him or his horse to eat. He pursued his course until he crossed Richland Creek near where the railroad crosses it without meeting any person or seeing a house. On the south side of the creek in a dense cane brake on the land now owned by David T. Reynolds he found a deer hung up and freshly skinned and some portions of it taken away. He got down and cut off a piece and broiled it on a fire which he struck up, but could not eat it without salt or bread. It made him sick. Believing that those who killed the deer could not be far off he commenced hollering, and was answered by the surveying party who were not far from him. On getting to their camp he found them lying down and resting, as he thought, but as they remained longer idle than he supposed they would, he asked if they were not going on with the line. They told him it was Sunday and they did not work on Sunday; he assured them it was not Sunday, but before they could be satisfied they examined the memorandum of their travels, and found they had lost a day. Bright received from Anderson his location and notes of vacant land he had found on the trip and Bright went back to Nashville and had the lands before the party got back. Among the lands thus saved by Anderson was the Patterson tract adjoining Pulaski. The owners and holders of warrants and land claims were dissatisfied with the settlement and compromise of April, 1806 Between the State of Tennessee and the United States Government, requiring all warrants not located to be located North and East of the reservation line. They insisted that in 1783 the State of North Carolina after assigning new boundaries to the Cerokee Indians in East Tennessee appropriated all other vacant land in the State, whether claimed by Cherokees or Chickasaw Indians to the redemption of her public debt, and to satisfy the claims of her officers and soldiers; that a large portion of the warrants were issued in exchange for special certificates of indebtedness, and that such warrants were received under the assurance that the holders had the right to locate them on any vacant land in the State. That at that time North Carolina was an independent sovereign State with all her rights and sovereignty that Great Britain possessed; that by the Act of cession the U. S. Government took the territory subject to the satisfaction of the warrants and was bound to fulfill in good faith all the just obligations of the State of North Carolina to her own citizens in relation to said territory. That by restricting warrant holders to but little over one-half the State and withholding a porition of that for schools was impairing the obligation of the original contract between the State of North

Carolina and her own citizens and was inequitable and unjust to the warrant holders. Such was the dissatisfaction that the legislature of Tennessee appointed a Commission of which General Strother was chief to ascertain whether there was sufficient vacant lands of suitable quality North and East of the reservation line to satisfy the warrants not located. Soon after the cession in February, 1796, Congress stopped the entering of lands and prohibited those who had obtained grants for lands to which the Indian title had not been extingished from going on their lands or having them surveyed, or their lines marked. Many members of Congress from States that had no lands to cede, took the ground that all the entries made and grants issued on lands to which the Indian title had not been extinguished were void, embracing nineteen-twentieths of the whole State. This view of the question was agitated for twenty-five years, and caused great uneasiness to those whose interests were affected by it. Governor McMinn in his message to the Legislature in September 1817, refers to it, and says in substance, that the U. S. Government had granted six hundred and forty acres of land for the County-seat of Giles County, situated at Pulaski; and in many other respects acted as though they held those lands by regular title. That the United States Government claimed to hold under the cession from North Carolina, and if it acquired title from North Carolina it followed that the officers and soldiers had an indisputable right to the lands granted to them before the cession. Mr. Grundy in a speech in the United States Senate in 1812, urged the early extinguishment of the Indian title to the lands West of Maury and Giles, embracing the Western and South-western part of Giles, and to the Mississippi river. It was charged that the delay was unnecessary; that by postponing the establishment of lines until the original locators and surveyors were dead or removed, the claimants would be unable to identify their lands.

In this way many persons lost their lands, and others were compelled to litigate their titles. For twenty years after Giles was first settled there was almost a continuous litigation of land claims; and but for the eminently wise and conservative policy of our Courts, in adjusting and quieting titles, the loss would have been much greater. But the equitable and liberal administration of our land laws could not reach the loss to the poor soldiers to whom the warrants were issued; many of them had no homes, their pay and their subsistance for the greater portion of their six years hard service were in land warrants; a considerable portion of which were entered, and grants issued to the owners before 1790, but they could not occupy them. The delay and indifference manifested by Congress, disheartened them and depreciated Western lands, and land warrants. The necessities of the owners and holders forced them to sell for whatever they could get; and in this way speculators and capitalists became largely possessed. As an evidence of it one among the first deeds registerd in our County, was by parties in Philadelphia for 226,260 acres, made up of various tracts in different parts of the State, many of which were in Gilees County.

CHAPTER VII—DEPOSITION OF GEN. JAMES ROBERTSON

The party of citizens that went out to Latitude Hill in 1783, on their return camped the first night on Haywood Creek, where Elisha Robertson located a tract of five thousand acres of land for John Haywood, describing the land as beginning on a white oak one mile above a large spring on the bank of a small creek that runs into Richland, which the Commissioners and their guard came down on their return from Elk River, and on which they camped the first night.

This was the land on which Albert Buford now lives. Either because of the indefinite description of the land, or fear of litigation, the depositions of T. Cox and General James Robertson were taken on the 10th of February 1809, under the orders of the County Court of Maury County, to identify the land, perpetuate testimony, etc. General Robertson identified the land very satisfactorily. Richard Hightower, Gideon and Wm. Pillow and Wm. P. Anderson were present, and asked a number of questions, among others who were along,—the object of the expedition, and the route traveled. In answer to which he gave the names of such as he had remembered, and described their travel; as these were the first white men who explored the County, and as many of their descendents are still living in the County, I will give the names of those who were along and substance of the deposition

He states that sixty or eighty persons were along, their names as far as he remembers were: Anthony Bledsoe, Kasper Mausker, Daniel Smith, Isaac Bledsoe, Philemon Thomas, Elijah and James Robertson, Frederick Stamps, Thomas Cole, John Lackey, Andrew Casselman, Benjamin Casselman, Wm. Davis, Davidson, William Doggans, Andrew Boyd, two by the name of Shelby, three by the name of McMurray, O. McCutcheon, Samuel McCutcheon, James McCutcheon, J. Hollis, Turner and Sampson Williams, James Clendener, D. Frazier, Robert Banks, E. McLain, Jamees Sanders, William Callensworth, D. Hays, Jas. Todd, Thomas Spencer, John Gibson, Edward Cox, Wm. Bradshaw and N. McClure.

He states in substance that they started from Nashville in February, 1783, that leaving the Commissioners, Isaac Bledsoe and A. Tatum, and the balance of the guard at the Harpeth Glades, on the Big South road, they set out South to ascertain the Southern boundary of the State, and to hunt a body of good land, to run out General Greene's 25,000 acres somewhere South of the line the Commissioners were running. They camped the first night between Harpeth and Flat Creek, about two miles from Duck River, and crossed Duck River at what was called the Shallow Ford and encamped the second night on what they called Floating Camp Creek, now called Cedar Creek; third night on Robertson Fork, fourth night on a branch of Bradshaw Creek, the next night on Bradshaw, stopping before twelve o'clock to take their latitude, and stayed there two or three nights. They were then one or one and a half miles from mouth of the creek. Rain fell that night so as to raise the Elk River past fording. The next morning they went to Elk, going about two miles, and struck the river where McCutcheon's trace crossed it. Gen. Daniel Smith took the observations, and concluded they were in about three miles of the South boundary of the State. Their purpose was to make a canoe and send some of the party over to ascertain the Southern boundary; but there being a good deal of fresh Indian signs and Indian horses, they concluded not to cross the river, but to turn back after marking a number of trees, which place is now known by the marked trees, where McCutcheon's trace crossed Elk River. (The place is on a high bluff on the North-side of the river, and is now called

Latitude Hill.) States that they aimed to go South from the
Harpeth Glades but at times discovered that they were off the
course. They took observations several times; some of the
names of the company were generally cut upon the trees at
each encampment. The weather was very cold and they cut
not less than a dozen trees at each encampment for fire wood.
Elijah Robertson named Robertson Fork, and probably Haywood. Gen. Robertson himself named Richland Creek. Bradshaw and Indian Creeks were named but does not state who
named them. After they left the marked trees at Elk river they
went up Indian Creek, over to and up Buchanan Creek out to
and down Haywood, where they camped the first night; over
to and down Fountain Creek to near the fork where they
camped the second night. From there they went a North-western course to the mouth of Little Bigby, and run out General
Greene's twenty-five thousand acres on the South side of
Duck River, including the mouth of Little Bigby.

SETTLERS ON INDIAN LANDS DRIVEN OFF

In 1809, 1810 and 1811, U. S. Soldiers from Fort Hampton
situated on Elk River four miles above its mouth, were sent
out in the month of June to drive all the setlers off the Indian
land as it was called, although some of the settlers had grants
for their land. They acted very rascally; cut down the corn
with large butcher knives, threw down and burned fences
and houses and forced the settlers back over the line. In some
localities the settlers soon returned, and the villianous work
of removal and destruction of improvements was repeated.
This was a terrible calamity on the settlers who, had strug-
gled against so many difficulties to get places on which to
live. In the prospect of rising corn for their bread, the most
of those driven off went back over the line, and built huts
and camps on the land of any one who would permit them to
do so. They had to do this or anything to shelter their families until they could do better. Among those driven off were
the following: William Welch, who lived six or seven miles
West of Campbellsvill, was driven off and his improvements
and crop were destroyed. Lawson Hobson's improvements
and crop were totally destroyed, and his hands driven off.
Robert Reed had inadvertently built his cabin on the line;

the soldiers would not allow it to remain, and threatened to burn it, but gave him permission to remove it. Charlees W. Dever who lived on the place now owned by Mrs. Lindsay was driven off and his extensive improvements and crop was destroyed. Levy Reed, Esq., says he saw six houses burning at one time on the banks of Weakley Creek by United States Soldiers, because they were on the Indian side of the line. Thomas Reed, Sr., who livd about a quarter of a mile East of where J. P. C. Reed now lives, was on Indian territory and his crop and improvements were destroyed, cut down and burned

In the neighborhood of Prospect a good mny persons were over the line, and they were treated as those on Weakley Creek, many of them went back over the line and built cabins and camps on the Ward tract of land. James Ford kept a little ferry on Elk at the mouth of Fords Creek, and the United States Government had contracted with him to ferry over the mail-rider who carried the mail from Columbia to Fort Hampton once every two weeks, was permitted to remain until his contract went out, and the very day it expired the soldiers came and threw down his fence and took the roof off his house. Ford moved back a few miles and rented land for three years before he returned. A good many families on Shoal Creek and West of Prospect were driven off at the same time; among them were Reuben Riggs and Henry E. Morgan, who lived on the Carey Gilbert place; William Noblett, James McKinney, Kallett Nail and others lived over the line, were visited by the soldiers, and the crops and improvements of most of them were destroyed. On the South side of the river William Kyle had a large and valuable farm, and he was driven off three times. On the Alabama side the Reduses and Simmses and those who settled Simms' settlement, were driven off and they went back over the line and built camps and shanties which they covered with bark which they stripped from the trees like tan bark. A considerable number of these camps were together, and the place was called Barksville for a long time. I saw the camps with the bark covers on them when a boy.

INDIAN ALARMS

The early settlers lived for several years and until after the close of the war of 1812 in constant fear of the Indians. This was especially so in the Western and Southern portion of the County. It will be borne in mind that the Chickasaw Indians' boundary line until September, 1816, ran from Lewis' Grove at the South-west corner of Maury County to Ditto's landing on the Tennessee River, and approached to within five miles of Pulaski, and crossed Elk River two or three mils above Prospect, leaving the West and South-western portion of the County in Indian territory.

All the country West, South-west and South of that line, for hundreds of miles belonged to the Indians. Three miles above Ditto's landing on a line to the head of Elk, and thence to the head of Duck River, and from thence to the mouth of the Hiawassee on the Tennessee River, all South and East for hundreds of miles was claimed by the Cherokee Indians, until February, 1819, thus giving the Indians both banks of the Tennessee River, from the mouth of the Hiawassee to the mouth of Duck River, except eight miles on the North side at Ditto's landing secured to the whites by the treaties of 1805 and 1806. In all the territory thus claimed by them they roamed and hunted at pleasure, and passed through the country to and from their excursions to Northern tribes; and even by the treaty of 1805, they were allowed to hunt North and East of said line for some time. The proximity of the early settlers to the Indians, and their frequent appearance in numbers sufficient to be formidable, in their hunting and traveling excursions, together with a knowledge of the cruelties perpetrated by them, on the early settlers on the Cumberland and other places; their character for treachery, ambuscade and stealthy approach, the sparse population and dense cane brakes, which covered the whole country, all contributed to keep up a state of uneasiness and dread of the Indians. And besides, during the war of 1812, it was generally believed that there were British and Spanish emigrants among the Indians encouraging them to acts of hostility. Frequently, reports from trivial circumstances, were circulated, that the Indians were hostile in feeling and meditated an attack; and some times that they were approaching. On such occasions the settlers in the Southern and Western part of the County would go back into the settlements, and remain a few days. The terror and confusion of whole families in flight from a supposed hostile advance of Indians, is absolutely indescribable.

I witnessed several of these flights when a boy. My father lived about ten miles from the nearest point to the Indian line. He never left home, but two or three times made preparations to go, hid his valuables, and had his horses and wagon ready. One time the settlers South of my father went back to Gordon's twelve miles North-east of where we lived. At another time they went back to the Reverend Alx McDonald's five miles North-west.

On such occasions those who would remain would assemble three or four families at the strongest and most secure house in the neighborhood, and prepare for defense. At night they would carry the axes into the house, stretch chains across the door to keep the door shutters from being broken in suddenly, load their guns, have their butcher knives close at hand, select their cracks in the house to be used as portholes, put down the fire—and one man would sit up as sentinel while the others slept.

At one time in the Fall of 1813, soon after the terrible massacre at Fort Mimms, the settlers were greatly alarmed, especially in the Southern portion of the County. It was reported the Indians were certainly advancing; had crossed the State Line, and had killed one person. Such was the alarm that all the families South of my father's left home in great haste, not waiting to get up members of their families who were in the neighborhood, some in wagons, some on horseback, taking with them such of their valuables as they could conveniently carry. For a whole day they passed my father's going back into the settlements. My father, although he had made preparations to leave was quite unwilling to go, as long as any others would remain. Late in the evening three or four families residing immediately South of my father's came, and camped for the night. That night my father and three other neighbors, and those who had camped for the night, agreed to remain until more definite news could be obtained. In the morning they with several others started out to reconnoiter the Southern border of the County, and finding no Indians crossed the Tennessee River, and returned in a few days with the news that-the Indians had no hostile intentions. The alarm was first given by a young man in the Southern part of the County, who had killed another and immediately fled; and to prevent being pursued told every person he saw that the Indians were coming, had crossed the State Line, and had killed one person (the one he had killed himself,) and in this way the murderer escaped. The news reached Pulaski in the evening, and caused great alarm among the women and those few unused to Indian warfare; the men resolutely preparing to make a desperate defense. Immediately preparations were made for the battle. After dark the women and children and negroes were removed a mile East of town, and hid in a dense cane brake, on what is know called McKimmon's branch, two or three hundred yards East of Colonel Solon E. Rose's residence, and left there with strict orders to be perfectly quiet, and to keep the children from making a noise. The men then returned to meet the Indians when they advanced, resolved to exterminate or be exterminated.

All the dogs in town followed to the women and children's camp, and not having the fear of the Indians before their eyes, or caring for military orders; and being instigated by their canine instincts, they kept up an incessant barking and fighting all night, and could have been heard for miles around to "the great terror of the good people then and there assembled."

THE EARLY SETTLERS

Character, Habits, Their Mode of Life, Manners and Customs

The early settlers traveled the roads opened by previous emigrants to the point nearest the place they wished to go to, and then cut the cane at the place they stopped at. The cane on the rich lands was from twelve to twenty feet high, and on the ridges and thin land from four to seven feet high. The emigrant stopped frequently in the midst of a cane-brake, by a spring, cleared away the cane from a few rods of ground, erected a temporary shelter for his family, and then put up a log cabin, split out puncheons for the floor, the door-shutters were made out of long, wide boards, pegged on battons, and hung with wooden hingees. The chimneys were made of sticks and clay, generally very wide. The table was made out of slabs or boards, planed or drawn with a drawing knife.

The cupboard in one corner to the right or left of the fire place, made of the same material, and very rough. The bedsteads were made in the simplest and rudest style. The cradles for the children were made out of like material. Sometimes a sugar trough served the purpose, or the bark from a Hickory or Lynn tree, taken off in the Spring with a head and foot piece. Many of our brave ancestors were soothed to sleep in such a cradle in their infant days. There were no nails or plank to be had in the country; a chopping axe, (and sometimes a broad axe,) a frow, iron wedge, drawing knife, and hand saw, an auger and one or two chisels, occasionally a jackplane, were the mechanical tools of the early settlers, and with these he made every thing. Occasionally a settler would bring a cross-cut saw, and it was loaned for six or eight miles around. A few years later the whip-saw was brought in and plank sawed by hand for particular uses. Such was the indispensible out-fit of an early settler, together with his trusty rifle and keen butcher-knife, with which they were expert.

For the women it was equally indispensable to have a cotton spinning wheel and cards, and occasionally a flax wheel; and also a loom on which to weave cloth. The looms and everything were made in the rudest and most primitive style imaginable, and for want of house-room the looms were often set up at the end of the house outside, and covered by a shelter of boards. Deer, bear, panthers, wolves, wildcats, etc., were abundant, scarcely a day passing without seeing or hearing these animals. The men were all hunters, from necessity. In this way they provided meat for their families until they could raise hogs. The women made all the clothing, carded, spun, and knit, every night until bed time, and when the men and boys were not otherwise engaged, of nights, they picked the seed out of the cotton for mother; the women preferring to spin the cotton picked by hand. They spun and wove clothing for their husbands and sons, dyed the thread or wool with home-grown indigo, or with the bark and roots of various trees. The also spun and wove their own clothing.

It was very rare to see either man or woman with apparel that was made of imported goods. In addition to scarcity of goods and difficulty of procuring them, Giles County was settled soon after the restrictions on trade by the British Government know as "the orders in Council," followed by the "Milam Decrees," and then by the embargo of Congress in December 1807, and finally by such restrictions as almost prohibited all trade. And such was the opposition to Great Britain, that the wearing of imported goods or using anything imported, was deemed a disgrace and unpatriotic. An incident illustrative of the times was told of the grandmother of Mrs. Kercheval. A gentleman from one of the Eastern States at breakfast, playfully remarked that the coffee, (which was made of rye or okra, as was common in that day,) smelled very strong of the embargo. The lady replied with spirit that it smelled equally as strong of liberty. Such were the patriotic feelings that pervaded all classes, that they cheerfully submitted to hardships and privations to sustain the action of our Government, and maintain its precious honor. Very little imported coffee, tea, or sugar was used. Coffee was made of okra, rye, parched corn, etc.

The Bohea tea plant, a species of black tea, and cultivated and used by those fond of tea; it grew very well, and doubtless would yet. Sassafras tea was a favorite tea, and is still used very largely by people in the country. Large quantities of sugar was annually made from the sugar tree; every family made enough for family use, and same made it for sale. Molasses from the sugar tree, of a very fine quality, was made for family use. Every family had a sugar camp, where they boiled the water that ran from the trees; each family having from fifty to one hundred trees tapped and running at a time.

They lived almost entirely on corn bread. The Johnny cake, baked on a board about sixteen inches long, was a favorite mode of preparing it, and it tasted excellent.

The costume of the men and boys was generally the hunting shirt. It was comfortable and convenient for laboring men and easily made. It was worn by our soldiers during the Revolutionary War and was the militia uniform, and the early settlers cherished it for its associations. In the war of 1812 it was the uniform or most usual dress of the militia and volunteers from Tennessee. It is said that no troops impress a beholder with more awe, than a company of stout, athletic men, uniformed in the old-fashioned black hunting shirt. After the battle of New Orleans, it was inexplicable to Europeans how the flower of the British army was so easily defeated by undisciplined troops. A British soldier who was in the battle, on his return to England, was asked what kind of troops they encountered. He said they were large, strong-looking men, perfectly fearless, who wore black gowns, and had long black guns; and when they went to shoot they peeped along the top of their guns.

The early settlers tanned their own leather in troughs made for the purpose, and dressed the skins of deer killed by them, and made buck-skin, out of which hunting shirts, pants and vests were made for men and boys. They made their own shoes, their bridles and harness; often, at night, when the day's work was over, by the light of a candle or grease lamp, the boys would pick cotton, or reel thread for their mothers and sisters. The mother and girls would card, spin or knit until bed-time. This was all done in the same cabin. One great advantage to the children was, they heard all the conversations of their parents, and between them and grown-up persons who might be there as visitors, or so-journing for the night. They heard the tone of voice and saw the expression of countenance of their parents, when they condemned what they thought wrong, or praised virtuous and meritorious acts; and in this way the parents instilled into their children their own views of right and wrong by their daily life and actions before them; and left their impress upon them to a degree that cannot now be done, when the children spend most of their time in rooms to themselves. If children had school lessons to learn at night, they studied them in the room where their parents were, and the lesson was talked about and the children greatly assisted.

Again, children thus raised in the company of grown-up persons, hearing them talk about all subjects, their ideas were enlarged and more early matured; men were more communicative to boys, and more companionable; but the boys were quite different from what they generally are at present time. They treated boys like they thought they knew something. In this one respect the children of the first settlers were better off than the children of the present day, and makes one wish for the old times again.

Whilst the want of house room occasioned some inconvenience, it was not without advantages. Very little surplus fuel and candles were wasted by young men sitting up with the girls until mid-night. Young men then were men, and they meant business when they went to see the girls, and it did not take them very long to tell it and receive an answer. The fire-place was generally six or seven feet wide; the old folks would sit on one side and the young folks on the other; and if there was a couple that wanted to court, they sat next to the corner and the other young folks, between them and the old folks. Some of the best and most effective courting that ever was done in the County, was carried on with the old folks on one side of the fire-place, and the parties courting on the other.

When a new-comer arrived all the neighbors assembled to help build his house; and if it was late in the Spring and he was likely not to get enough ground cleared, on which to raise his bread-corn, the neighbors all put in a day or two chopping or making rails for him. When any of these settlers had a house to raise, or logs to roll, the neighbors went to help him, and very often their wives would go too, and have a quilting or sewing for the wife of the man whose logs were rolled. In the evening after the labors of the day were over, the men would amuse themselves with athletic exercises, wrestling, jumping, etc., and sometimes after supper they would have a country dance, or perhaps the young people would play "Old Sister Phoebie," or "William Co-Trimble-Toe," and the old folks would sit around and tell how it was when they were young.

So that these times of generous and substantial help to neighbors, were made scenes of social enjoyment, and pleasure to those who performed the labor. Although the early settlers as a class were deficient in learning, such as is taught in schools they were remarkable for their practical common sense, and their almost unerring discrimination of character. They were practical judges of human nature, and were rarely mistaken. If a new-comer was honest, truthful, and industrious, and was not a coward, he had friends, and although he might have a fight at every muster, as long as he acted honorably and brave, he had friends; but if he showed the least proclivity to dishonesty or falsehood, or was lazy, he lost all claims to the sympathy of his neighbors; and if he was cowardly, that, of itself was looked on as little less than a crime. Men at that day fought when they were insulted; public opinion forced them to do t, without regard to whether they whipped or got whipped. But they fought with nature's weapons. It was a fist fight; and when over they made friends, took a drink and the past was forgotten.

A man who would then draw a pistol or dirk on his antagonist, would be ostracised, called a dirty coward, and lose all prestige of chivalry.

HOSPITALITY

The hospitality of the first settlers was proverbial; travelers had no difficulty in staying at any house where night overtook them, if they were willing to put up with the fare, such as the family enjoyed; their horses were cared for and they provided for, as comfortably as the circumstances of the family would enable them to do, without fee or reward, except those few on thoroughfares, who kept houses of entertainment as a means of living. No traveler was charged for a night's lodging. The entertainment, unostentatious and humgle as it may have been, was sa cordial, and every attention rendered so cheerfully, that if it was poor the traveler went away their friend, and if he was in search of land to buy, he felt as if he would like to be in that neighborhood.

DOMESTIC HABITS AND ECONOMY

It was a maxim of the first settlers to buy nothing they could produce or make themselves. No farmer sent to Nashville for seed potatoes or for wheat or oats to sow, these were produced in the County; and one neighbor got from another very often by an exchange of commodities. Mechanics in those days seldom laid in stock, but worked the material of their customers. The farmer furnished the iron and steel out of which his axes, plows and other tools were made, and the smth charged a certain price for his work. When boots, and shoes were made by a regular shoemaker, the leather and even the shoe thread was furnished by the customers, and the shoemaker charged for the making. Men and boys when they wanted fine hats, caught the raccoons, or got the requisite number of skins, and took them to the hatter and he charged a certain price for making. In this way a hat cost about twenty per cent less than to buy it, and the saving to the customer with the blacksmith and shoemaker, was in the same proportion. As late as 1840 I was in Mr. Thomas Martin's store, when he was showing Major James Buford some goods for negro clothing. Major Buford told him he had his negro clothing made at home. Mr. Martin replied that the labor of the negro woman would be worth more in the cotton field than it could be making cloth, and that it was cheaper to purchase the cloth. Major Buford replied that it might be so that year, but it would be breaking one of his long established rules "to buy nothing he could make himself." Major Buford was then and continued to be one of the largest and most successful farmers in the County. The first settlers raised their own rice and cleaned by beating in a mortar. They cultivated the Indigo plant and made their own Indigo, which was preferred by the old women who understood dyeing, to the Indigo of commerce. They raised their own flax, prepared it and had it spun for shoe thread or wove it into linen for the Summer wear for men and boys. They raised their own hemp and made their own rope.

The women were as economical and industrious as the men, and even more so. They made jeans, linseys, and cotton goods, knit socks, saved the feathers from their geese and ducks, made tree sugar, butter, cheese, tallow candles, soap and many other things, which they bartered in stores, for such goods and articles as they wanted; and many of them paid their entire purchases in this way. And it was not confined to them whose circumstances made it necessary for them to do so, but the wives of the most influential and wealthy prided themselves in paying all their own expenses. Like all noble women of their day they sought by domestic economy to keep down expenses, and better their estates. The most of families had their merchants with whom they traded, and had an understanding with them in relation to such articles as they expected to barter, and the women thought no more of sending their bater to their mechant, when it was ready or going with it themselves, than their husbands did in sending their bacon, wheat, hemp, and other farm products to the same merchant, often to be bartered for something else. The women made their own dresses and the clothing for their husbands and sons There were but few tailors and a considerable portion of their custom was in cutting out Sunday coats for men and boys, which were made at home. We had then no milliners or banks, and no use for either, as it took only six yards of calico to make a woman a dress, and there was little money in the country. But now they have both become indispensable, and the trouble is as to which shall have precedence. As to the habits of the young men I will give two incidents illustrative of the times.

I have heard Mr. Tom Martin often tell that when he was sixteen or seventeen years old, he went to live in a store as a clerk at seventy-five dollars per year and his board. He found his own clothing, which was made for him by his mother. At the end of the first year he had his seventy-five dollars, less three dollars and fifty cents, having spent only three dollars and a half during the year. He was the most successful merchant I ever knew, and he made a large fortune at the business. I heard Dr. P. W. Phelps, late of Elkton say, that during the first course of lectures he attended at Transylvania University,, he spent only two dollars more than his actual necessary board, tuition and traveling expenses. Is it surprising that such men succeeded?

MILLS—COTTON GINS AND OPERATIONS

The settlers who came the latter part of 1807 and 1808, and the early part of 1809, had great difficulty in procuring meal for bread, and even corn out of which to make the same. For the first two years a considerable portion of the meal used was packed on horses from Williamson County. Some beat their corn in mortars, others ground it on hand-mills. The first mill was built on Robertson's Fork by Nat Moody, about a half mile South of Lynnville Station. Robert Buchanan built a mill on Buchanan's Creek in 1809 which ground in the latter part of the year. About the same time Cunningham built a mill on Richland Creek near where S. B. March lives, and Hardy Hightower one on Bradshaw. John White built a mill on Robertson's Fork near Buford's Station at an early day. Baylor built a mill on Big Creek in 1809 or 1810, it was among the first mills in the County. Williams built a mill at a very early day on the South side of Elk River, on the Blowing Spring branch, near where Morrell's mill is now situated. Some of the settlers in the North-west part of the County, got their meal the first year or two at Pillow's mill on Little Bigby in Maury County. After the Town of Pulaski was laid off, Nat Moody moved to Pulaski and built a mill on Richland Creek, about 1811 or 1812; and about the same time a mill was built on the creek below Mount Moriah Church, opposite where James Hays lives called Mayfield's or Clack's Mill. Besides these there were horse-mills in different neighborhoods which were indispensable for grinding in summer, as most of the mills that were first built were on streams that failed in summer.

Many of the frst emigrants brought with them cotton seed, and at first planted small patches, like garden patches, then half an acre and some times more, gradually increasing as they opened land. It was raised for several years in this way for home consumption. Little was raised for market until after the war of 1812. The first sold on the market was in small parcels, generally sold in the seed. George Malone on Lynn Creek and Thomas Meredith, who lived four miles South of Pulaski, on what is now the Rodes farm, were the first who raised in any considerable quantity for market.

The first settlers separated the lint from the seed with their fingers; some used two rollers, one above the other turned by a crank. In 1810 or 1811 Lester Morris who lived near Rehoboth Church, made a small gin turned by hand, a year or two later he made a large one that was operated by one horse, with which he ginned for his neighbors several years. John Laird started the first gin that was run by water in 1811 or 1812 on Lynn creek; about the same time or soon after, John Henderson started one on a branch about a mile South of Cornersville. Col. Hulburt started one on Dry Creek at an early day, near where Colonel Wheeler now lives. This was about 1813. Cotton gins were used in Madison County before they were in Giles. I remember when a small boy my father took a few hundred pounds of seed cotton to a gin in Madison County on Flint River; the next year he took it to Calloway's gin. For packing cotton Calloway had a large hole cut in the floor, and dropped the empty bag through it, fastened the mouth of the bag to the floor, and pressed the cotton with the feet and with mauls. In this way he packed in large long bags about 250 pounds.

John Laird had a square box made, and put the bag or cloth in the box, tramped the cotton in with the feet or pummeled it with mauls or pestles. It was several years before cotton was packed by lever power. Great improvement has been made in the cultivation of cotton. It was a disputed question with the early settlers whether there was any advantage derived from thinning it in the stand. The first cotton I ever saw raised was not thinned and the first I ever saw thinned was left, a stalk to the foot, scattered over the top of the drill two inches wide. William Brown, Esq., was the first in the Southern part of the County who tried chopping through it with the hoe, and he was persuaded to make the experiment by old Mr. Strong, who had cultivated cotton or had seen it cultivated in the South.

TOBACCO

The first settlers commenced raising tobacco as they did cotton, for their own consumption. Those who came from the State of Virginia were acquainted with the cultivation of it, and preferred it as a crop to cotton. The land was new and rich and better adapted to tobacco, than cotton. From 1816 to 1821 a large quantity of tobacco was shipped annually from Giles. Under an Act of the Legislature, the County Court appointed Inspectors for Pulaski and Lower Elkton at the mouth of Richland Creek, the two points from which tobacco was mostly shipped. About 1820 or 1821 the price declined until it barely paid the expenses of shipping, and then the cultivation of it was abandoned.

HEMP

From 1811 to the close of the war, there was a good deal of hemp raised in the County. It brought a good price during the war. Those who raised it sent it to Nashville, and generally brought back salt.

CATTLE

But for several years after the first settlers came, and until the close of the war more money was realized from the raising of cattle than from any other business.

The range was good and the cattle required nothing but salting occasionally, and a little attention to keep them from straying off. Beef cattle were in great demand during the war. Some of the early merchants collected their accounts in beef cattle, and drove them to Baltimore, and with the proceeds purchased their goods. I remember that Mr. Doren was one that purchased goods in that way.

MERCHANTS

The first merchants for many years went to Baltimore on horseback for their goods, and their goods were hauled out on wagons from Baltimore. Some goods were occasionally brought up the river in keel boats from New Orleans. From the early settlement of the country until about 1840, numerous flat-bottomed boats were built at Pulaski, and at various points along Richland Creek and Elk River, by which the tobacco, cotton, hemp and other products were shipped to market; generally shipped to New Orleans.

These boats floated down with the current, and usually required about six weeks to make the descent; under favorable circumstances it was made in less time, dependent upon the stage of the water and the influence of the winds. For inexperienced boat hands about fifty dollars was paid for the trip. The hands received their wages in New Orleans, and defrayed their own expenses home. The most of them walked home. Many young men who had never been out of the county availed themselves of this opportunity to see "the world." The marvelous stories they told on their return were listened to by the boys with as much interest as if they had made a made a tour to the Holy Land. At an early day keel boats were brought up the river with merchandise. The trip required between three and four months. Salt was brought down the Tennessee River from King's salt works in keels and piroques to the mouth of Elk, and up Elk to the mouth of Richland; occasionally up Richland to Pulaski; but generally stopped at the mouth of Richland, then called Lower Elkton, or went up to what is now Elkton.

MANUFACTURE OF POWDER

The most of the powder used by the first settlers for many years was manufactured in the County. The ingredients of which, as doubtless, all know, are Nitre, Charcoal and Sulphur, requiring, according to the French formula, seventy-five parts of Nitre and twelve and a half each of charcoal and sulphur. This formula is often varied. Daniel Allen, father of General R. H. Allen, erected a powder mill at a very early day at Allen's Spring, since known as Wright's Spring, a few miles North-west of Campbellsville. The salt-petre used by him was procured mostly from a cave near Campbell's Station in Maury County, which, at one time was worked by Dr. G. D. Taylor, also from a cave three-fourths of a mile South-west of Dr. Rutledge's old brick residence; which was worked by Gabriel and John Foulkes, who exchanged salt-petre for powder, and sold and bartered the powder in the neighborhood. A man by the name of Williams had a powder mill near the State Line, about one mile South-west from Elkmont Springs, on the Blowing Spring branch. Salt-petre was procured from two caves in the neighborhood, but mostly from a cave near the mouth of Elk River. A man named Manasco, living on Indian Creek, made excellent powder on a small scale, enough for the neighborhood. He was a Dutchman, and generally when asked if he had any good powder on hand, would say in his foreign brogue, he had some but it was not first-rate, it was a little too quick and a little too strong.

At a later day Jas. Ross had a powder mill in the Western part of the County. His was on the Lawrenceburg road. Some of the salt-petre used by him was procured from a cave in Wayne County. The cave near the mouth of Elk River was extensively worked for a number of years, and afforded employment for many persons living in the Southern part of the County.

Potash was in great demand during the war. It was used in lixerating and chrystalizing the salt-petre. Many persons engaged in the business who procured ashes from log-heaps, burned and otherwise, dripped them and boiled the lye down to a black salt, or sort of residium, which they sold to those who were making salt-petre.

In the Southern part of the County many young men and

lads went through the woods, and put fire in all the hollow trees they could find with a hole near the ground, and one near the top of the tree. The blaze would run out at the top and roar like distant thunder. The ashes or rather cinders secured in this way, were said to be richer in potash than ashes procured from a burning log-heap. Many of the hollow trees now standing in the woods, that appear to have been burnt out, were burnt out in this way.

CHURCHES

Baptist—The first Baptist Church organization was at Crosswater in 1808 or 1809, by the Buchanans and Ezells. The church building was a log house on a glade about a quarter of a mile South of the Spring. George Brown and William Calloway were the preachers. After the removal of the Buchanans and Ezells from the neighborhood, the place of worship was changed and another house erected, near Lewis B. Marks' called "Old Zion."

The Lynn Creek Church near Old Lynnville was organized in November, 1810. John Martin was the first pastor, Jacob Baylor, Deacon.

The Robertson Fork Church about 1810 or 1811, Peter Ussery and Wm. James were among the first members.

A church was organized near the place now owned by A. R. Gordon, known as the Marin B. Woods' place as early as 1811. Willis Hopwood was the first preacher.

Indian Creek Church was organized in 1811. Mrs. Nathan Bass and Mrs. Wm. Watson were baptized and joined the church in 1811. George Brown was the first pastor; Samuel McKnight was among the first members. Wm. B. Brooks and Arnold Zealnor, a few years later were prominent members.

A Baptist Church was organized in Pulaski at a very early day, but neither the date nor first members can be ascertained.

Methodist—The first Methodist Church was organized on Lynn Creek, and about one and one-half miles North of Old Lynnville in 1808. A man named Prewitt was the first preacher. A church was organized in the neighborhood of Mount Pisgah in 1809, soon after the Reverend Alex McDonald came to the county The first meetings were held at his house. About the time a church was organized at Mt. Pisgah or soon after, one was organized in the neighborhood of Brick Church, but at what place or the date of the organization has not been ascertained. Alex McDonald preached to them occasionally.

A church was organized at Rehoboth at a very early day, about 1810 it is believed. The first meetings were held at the house of Lewis Brown. A church was organized at an early day on Indian Creek, at the house of old Thos. Stanford, about three miles South-west of the present Bee Spring Church, as early as 1810 or 1811. A Methodist Church was organized in Pulaski at a very early day, but the date has not been ascertained.

Presbyterian—The first Presbyterian Church organization was the Elk Ridge Church, two and a half miles East of Lynnville Station, by Reverend Gideon Blackburn and Robert Henderson. Hugh King, Jas. Shields, and others were Elders. David Weir was the first pastor. About the same time or soon after Mars Hill Church was organized, with William Black, Ephraim Patrick and others as elders.

Cumberland Presbyterian—Mount Moriah Church was organized in the Fall of 1811. Reverend Jas. B. Porter was the first pastor, and Major Hurlston, Thos. Ruby, Reese Porter and Jonathan Berry elders.

CAMP MEETINGS

The Presbyterians held a camp meeting near Elk Ridge Church in 1811, and established a camp ground and kept it up many years.

The Cumberland Presbyterians held a camp meeting and established a camp ground at Mt. Moriah, in the Fall of 1811, and kept it up until about the commencement of the late war.

The Methodists held a camp meeting in the neighborhood of Mt. Pisgah in the Fall of 1811, about a quarter of a mile East of where Wm. Oliver lives, and near where Major Mc-Donald lived at that time. The next year it was held on Pisgah Hill, where it was kept up until the late war. This was the most noted camp ground in Tennessee and was attended by people from a great distance. About 1830 there were over one hundred camps on the ground, and at some meetings from 150 to 200 perosns were reported as having professed religion. During the revival of 1817, Robert Paine, (now Bishop Paine,) Sterling and Hartwell Brown, professed religion that fall; and in a few weeks joined Conference and commenced preaching. They were well educated for that day, and soon took a high stand in the ministry, and were successful and useful preachers.

Several camp grounds were established at a later date, which flourished for a time but none lasted as long, or had the wide reputation of the three above mentioned. Camp meetings commenced with the very first settlements. They were a necessity of the times. There were but few church organizations. The first settlers, although but few of them were members of any church, were, as a class firm believers in the Christian religion, and had a great reverence for the Bible and the preaching of the Gospel. They would go to a great distance to hear preaching and on account of the sparse population, when there was an opportunity to hear preaching for several days, those who lived at a distance cooked their provisions, took bedding and went in wagons with their families prepared to stay several days. The first year they usually took their tent clothes, or made temporary camps. In this way they remained on the ground during the meeting. The next year the preparations made were more extensive and continued to increase, until, in some measure they became places of entertainment, and while, doubtless, they continued to do good, the necessity which brought them in to existence, does not now exist.

A peculiarity which attended these camp meetings has long since passed away. The "bodily exercise" or "jerks," which, more or less attended all revival meetings, from 1815 to 1825 were very frequent. Persons deeply affected upon the subject of religion, generally women and girls, were taken suddenly with spasms or convulsions, and, most generally severe jerkings of the head, so that the hair of the women and girls when unbraided, would crack like a whip. On such occasions the men in company would usually take hold of them, to keep them from injuring thmselves. It certainly was not pretense on the part of those who had these spasms. Girls that I could ordinarliy hold with one hand, and whose physical strength was not equal to half my strength, I could not begin to hold on such occasions without help. On one occasion at Old Stanford's a young woman took the jerks; the preaching was in the house where the family lived, and had their cooking utensils. Two young men were holding her when a very wicked man standing by told them to let her go that she had more sense than to fall among the pots, and said he saw her look that way when she was about to fall. He went out into the yard cursing and swearing when he, himself, took the jerks, which frightened him terribly. Whilst the jerks attacked persons under great excitement, most generally at religious meetings, there was no more religion in the jerks, as such, than in a hard ague. It was a sort of epilepsy, brought on frequently by symypathy with those who were exercised; it was contagious in the sense that epilepsy is said to be in the East India army where if one soldier is stricken down with it and it is generally known in the line, others are apt to be similarly affected, when, if it is concealed no others may be affected.

SCHOOLS

The first classic school outside of the Academy at Pulaski, was established by the Reverend Daniel Weir, near the junction of Lynn Creek and Robertson's Fork, between 1810 and 1815, and was kept up for many years. At this school a good many young men were taught the Latin and Greek language.

EARTHQUAKES

The earthquakes in the latter part of 1811 and first part of 1812, greatly alarmed many of the early settlers. They occurred about the time of the great shakes at New Madrid, which commenced in the Fall of 1811, and continued until the destruction of the City of Caracas, in South America, the twenty-sixth of March, 1812; after which they suddenly ceased. About New Madrid and on White River and on the Mississippi River from the mouth of the Ohio to the St. Francis, there was an incessant quaking for several months, in which the ground rose and sunk in great undulations, and the surface of the earth burst open in fissures, from which mud water was thrown as high as the tops of the trees; and in the time Reelfoot and other lakes were formed. The same great convulsion which caused the shakes at New Madrid, doubtless caused the quaking of the earth in this County. I have been unable to find any record of the shakes in this County. Mrs. Thomas Williams, now eight-seven years old, says the first shake here was on the 16th day of December, 1811. Dr. Henry Laird who was then ten years old, and living with his father at Old Lynnville, says the hardest shake was the 23rd of December, 1811. Others think that the hardest shake was in the Spring, in log-rolling time. Levi Reed, who was then twelve years old, remembers two hard shakes, one at night and the other in the morning, in which horses became so frightened that they ran away with a wagon. James L. Henry says the hardest shake was in December, 1811, on a Sunday night just before Christmas. He was then a man grown and in Pulaski at the time. From what I heard my parents relate and from others who were here at the time, there were several hard shakes at intervals; with a good many lighter ones. Horses, dogs and cows, by instinct, or probably from a change in the electrical condition of the atmosphere, seemed to have a premonition of an approaching shake and appeared restless and alarmed. The shakes were preceded by a low, rumbling sound, like a wagon going over a rough road-bed; or distant thunder; and sometimes they came suddenly without any warning. The shocks were sometimes like a sudden upheaving of the earth, and at other times the motion was vibrating or like a trembling of the ground. The dishes in the cupboard and the boards on the house would rattle.

Many persons became greatly alarmed on the subject of religion, and religious meetings were kept up in the neighborhood at intervals for several weeks, and at times for several days or nights in succession, as in times of a revival, at which some of the most religious were on the anxious seat, and some professed religion; but after the shakes were over many of those most alarmed, it is said were no better than they were before; and it was afterwards called by some in derision, "the Earthquake Revival." To show how powerfully some persons were wrought on by fear, I will relate an incident which I learned from my father. A man who lived a few miles from my father had been accused of making counterfeit money, and had been arrested and placed in jail a time or two; but who was never convicted, came to my father's the morning after the first hard shake, before he had heard the opinions of his neighbors, and told my father that he had buried some pieces of copper with other metals and some chemicals, to undergo a process, preparatory to making money out of it, and asked my father if that could have caused the shaking of the earth, and he made a clean breast of his plans, as if he had been confessing to a Priest, and wanted to get religion and be a better man than he had been. My father told him it was merely an earthquake and advised him to move off, which he did very soon after. I remember distinctly the first shake that I was told was an earthquake. It was early in the morning; the family had not risen from bed, my father had a wagon that was placed near the end of the house the shock was sudden and left the impression on my mind very much as if the corner of the house had been raised by a prize and suddenly dropped. The chains about the wagon rattled, and my father told me to run out and see what was about the wagon. I went out and returned and told him there was nothing. He then said it was an earthquake. I was alarmed and watched him to see if he was frightened, and finding that he was not alarmed, I soon got over it. I remember several shakes after that but nothing definite about them.

Thos Williams, an old citizen of this County, told me that he was on the Mississippi River in a flat-boat, near New Madrid when there was a hard shake, and at the time that Reelfoot Lake was formed, and other places were sunk. He said the cable of the boat was broken instantly and the boat carried up stream rapidly for near two hours, and that when they were running up stream the river behind them looked as if it had been greatly elevated, almost like a hill in the river behind them.

ANTIQUITIES

On the lands lately owned by the heirs of James Patterson, deceased, one and one-half miles East of Pulaski, and now owned by Governor John C. Brown, near his Western boundary, and near what was the boundary line or dividing line between the old Patterson tract and the Bernard M. Patterson tract, about three hundred yards South of the Fayetteville road, there were two Indian mounds; one forty feet at the base, and eight feet high, the other about thirty feet at the base and six feet high. Human bones were found in these mounds. No appearance where the earth thrown up was taken from. Large forest trees growing on them and around the base.

On the lands owned by L. D. Suttle, deceased, eight miles South-east of Pulaski on the place known as the Biles tract, on the East side of Richland Creek there was the remains of an ancient fortification. It was on high ground, might be called a hill, with a commanding view of all directions. On the side next to the creek it was steep; about thirty acres were enclosed, with an embankment five or six feet high, which, in 1826, before the land was cleared, was too high and steep to ride over it, except in places. The forest growth was large poplar, beech, etc., and trees three and four feet through were growing on the embankment and at the base of it. It was laid off with angles at particular places, and had the appearance of being planned by persons acquainted with military defenses, and must have been laid off by a people further advanced in civilization than the Aborigines of this country. On the lands lately owned by Doctor Ben Carter adjoining the town of Pulaski, about one hundred yards South of the well where the negro quarters were, was a mound about thirty feet at the base, and six or seven feet high; between the well and the mound is a branch, the bottom of which is a hard limestone rock, on one side is a rock ten or fifteen feet long and several feet wide, in which was the well defined track of a larg oxen, and a man with a moccasin on. The track of the oxen is two or three inches deep, and that of the man one and a half or two inches. Both tracts plain and distinct, as if made in soft clay. The mound is South-west of the railroad and near to it. The tracks are fifty or one hundred yards North-east of the mound.

CANNON BALL

In 1812 or 1813 a cannon ball was found by one of the negroes that belonged to Wm. Marr, in a dense cane-brake, at what is known as the panther spring, htree-quarters of a mile North-west of Marrs Hill Church, and about four and a half miles North-west of Cornersville. At the same time they found in a hollow tree at the spring a large number of rock arrow points.   The old McCutcheon trace passed near the spring.   The cannon ball is in my possession and weighs eleven and a half pounds, and is doubtless what was called a twelve pounder. When Mr. Marr moved from the County in 1818, he left the ball with Ephraim Patrick, who was a neighbor and it has remained in his family ever since, and was sent to me by his daughter, Mrs. Moffitt.   The inquiry naturally arises, how did the cannon ball come there? It may have been taken there by the Indians traveling from the settlements on the Cumberland, or the Commissioners who went out to Latitude Hill in 1783 may have had artillery with them and left it there.   They had a guard of soldiers and traveled the McCutcheon trace which was near where the ball was found. Or if Desoto crossed the Tennessee River as is insisted by some and is more than probable, that he did, it may have been left there by him.

On the East side of Richland Creek opposite the shoals, on a high bluff were the remains of an ancient fortification. About four acres were enclosed within the embankment, oblong in form and evidently designed for defense. The earth was thrown up and although beaten down considerably, was since the settlement about three feet high, and had the appearance of having had four entrances at unequal distances, one toward a spring in the bank of the creek. There were Indian graves within the enclosure. Kirk's house, where the first courts were held, was in the enclosure. In a cave at the spring known as Anderson's spring in the Northern part of the town, the bones of a remarkably large human were found. The jaw-bone would go over an ordinary man's jaw, and the thigh bone was a good deal larger than that of a very tall man. Some pieces of pottery were also found. The pottery was a composition of shells; some flint pikes were occasionally seen. High up in the cave a human body was discovered in a remarkable state of preservation, surrounded with a cloth in whichfeathers had been interwoven.   Numerous mounds and burying places exist in various parts of the County, which from the trees growing on and about them must have been made hundreds of years before the white people settled the country. A remarkable feature in some of those mounds is that they are built up of shells and pebbles, which must have been transported from a considerable distance from river or creek. Another remarkable feature in those burying places is the wonderful state of preservation in which the bones were found when first exhumed.

INCIDENTS AND ADVENTURES OF EARLY SETTLERS

The unwritten history of our County abounds in incidents of frontier life the narrative of which would perhaps excite the wonder and challenge the credulity of the present generation. No record has been made of them they live but in the memory of the few old settlers remaining and with them will soon pass away and be forgotten. Few of them perhaps, have any historic worth except as they serve to show prime traits of character. The early settlers were remarkable for their self-reliance and daring adventure, which were impressed on their descendants, and doubtless have had a great influence in moulding the character of our present citizens.

In illustration of these dominant traits of character, I will give a few incidents and adventures of the early settlers.

The noble women in that day were, in their sphere, fully equal to the men, and should not be forgotten. Mr. and Mrs. James Ford settled on the North bank of Elk River, near Prospect, in June, 1807. In the Fall of the year he went back to East Tennssee after his stock, leaving his wife and children the oldest of whom was a daughter twelve years old, by themselves. Whilst he was absent one of the childrn sickened and in the night died. Mrs. Ford dressed it and watched by it until day. In the morning having no one by whom she could send word to the neighbors, except her children, and fearing to send them off, the poor women left them with the dead child and went to Mr. Johnson's, her nearest neighbor about a mile off, on the same side of the river, traveling through a dense cane-brake with no road but a bridle-path, liable every moment to meet a bear or panther, or Indian. Arriving there she engaged Mr. Johnon to make the coffin. She then returned home and then went to Mr. Kyles, a neighbor on the other side of the river, having to wade the river, to get him to dig the grave. Such were the wives and mothers of the early pioneers. The oldest daughter of Mrs. Ford, now Mrs. Kerr, still

survives, (1875), and from her I recently received the foregoing incident, together with much valuable information as to
the early settlers.

The Bolins—In 1808 or 1809, the precise date not ascertained, but probably in 1809, a tragedy occurred at James
Ford's the father of Mrs. Kerr, of no ordinary character. It
was at a time when there were no courts or civil officers in
what is now Giles County, and must have therefore have been
before February, 1810, and it was after courts were established in Maury County, which was the latter part of 1807. A
man named Reynolds, who lived on the Thomas Reed place
on the river, and a man named Rarden, who lived at the Thos.
Witson place, arrested a young man named Crouch, at the
house of Bolins who lived one and a half miles West of Ford's
at what has since been called the Alex Brown place. Crouch
was a nephew of the Bolins, and Reynolds and Rarden arrested him in bed early in the morning, tied his hands and started
with him to Columbia, to have him tried or committed by the
legal authorities on a charge of felony, there being no courts
or civil officers in Giles. They stopped at Ford's to get breakfast, and it was before breakfast time. Ford met them and
asked them not to stop at his house, as the Bolins, the young
man's uncles were his neighbors, and were dangerous and
desperate men and he feared they might come up while the
men were at brakfast and have a difficulty, and they might
do him an injury. They insisted on having breakfast and got
down. Mrs. Ford who was in the yard tending to some domes
tic duties told her husband if they must have breakfast there
was plenty of cold victuals cooked and on the table, and to go
and give it to them and let them get off as soon as possible.
Before they got in the house the two Bolins came in, and advanced towards the young man. They all had their guns. Reynolds told Bolins not to interfere or he would shoot. One of
the Bolins cut or partially cut the rope that tied the young
man's hands and as he cut it Reynolds fired and immediately
Rarden and one of the Bolins shot. The three shots were almost simultaneous. The Bolin that cut the rope although shot
through, took his gun from his shoulder and shot Rarden as
he was turning to walk off, and killed him instantly. One of
the Bolins lived three or four hours and died; the other lived

until some time in the night. Reynolds' arm was broken and the bullet cut two or three holes in his vest. Rarden was buried at Ford's. The Bolins at the Alex Brown place, where they lived. The foregoing is the recollection of Mrs. Kerr about the killing, which took place at her father's when she was thirteen or fourteen years of age. Her account agrees with what I recollet myself to have heard the neighbors say about it. Rarden's grave was shown to me in 1826, by Capt. Baker P. Potts, and he related the circumstances as he had heard them from Ford. He stated that Reynolds attempted to load his gun again, got the powder down and started the ball, but by weakness from loss of blood and having the use of only one hand, he could not ram the bullet down, his gun being a rifle; and seeing the prisoner start off he begged Ford to ram the bullet down for him, that he might shoot the prisoner and offered him or his wife either one fifty dollars to ram the ball down for him, which they declined to do. The prisoner went off, Reynolds got well, and nothing was done with him about it.

Spencer Clack—Spencer Clack was born in the State of Virginia in 1783, and while a youth came with his father, Major John Clack, to Sevier County, in East Tennessee, where he remained several years and came with his father in 1807 or 1808 to this County. His father first settled one mile West of the Court House on the Dr. Carter farm near the well, at what was called the negro quarter. While living there Spencer with two white men and a negro man, ran a very large bear into a cave, the entrance to which was an opening like a sink-hole; and it was called the sink-hole cave. The descent was precipitous and difficult, and about ten feet from the top of the ground to the bottom of the cave. Clack knew the interior of the cave and the extent of it, as he had explored it before. The bear having evaded his pursuit several times before, he determined to kill it this time at any risk. He caused a rope to be fastened around each of his ankles to aid him in descending and to draw him back if it should become necessary, and after giving directions to the white men and the negro, with a torch in one hand and his gun in the other, he slowly descended head foremost. As soon as his head entered the cavity he shined the bear's eyes, and found he was off to one side about fifteen feet, and by the time he got to the bottom of the cave he could see the body of the bear standing with his side towards him. Being a good marksman, expert with the knife and an experienced bear hunter, he took his aim behind the shoulder so as to shoot him through the heart. He said he was fully satisfied when his gun fired that he had killed the bear dead and would have no trouble with him. He fastened the ropes to the bear and was drawn up by the men above.

Jesse Lamb—Jessie Lamb was one of the first settlers on Indian Creek. He was a small man of unusual strength and agility and an experienced bear hunter. On one occasion as was told me when I was a young man, he run a bear into a large hollow log then crawled into the log after the bear with his butcher-knife, knowing that the bear would make a rush to get out as soon as he found something was coming in after him. When Lamb heard the bear start he lay down with his face up, and as the bear was passing over him he stabbed him behind the shoulder and killed him instantly. On another occasion he became satisfied that a wolfe in the neighborhood had her whelps in a cave about a mile Northwest of where Jas. Paine lived. He went into the cave, found the old wolf out, got the young ones and carried them home.

Mr. Lavesk—Mr. Lavesk was one of the early settlers in the Southern part of the County. On one occasion he was traveling through an uninhabited portion of the country South of Elk River, on one of those trails or bridle- paths that preceded roads. In the evening he discovered a large panther following him. Being in doubt whether the panther was pursuing his journey on the highway, or pursuing him, he quickened his pace for some time, but noticed that the panther kept about the same distance from him. His only weapon of defense was a pistol. He could not rely on that except at a short distance, and then if he failed to kill he would have little chance to retreat. It was then nearly sun-down and he could not reach any house before dark. It became important to know whether the panther was pursuing him; and if so, to have the fight before dark. He came to a place where the road forked and came together again in a short distance. Lavesk took the path that was but little traveled and when the panther came to the fork he took the same path. He then decided the panther was pursuing him, and he at once selected the ground and planned the attack. There was a log across the path which he had to cross over and just beyond and close to the path a tree blown up. He got off the horse and moved him out of the path. Then he cocked his pistol and dropped on his knees by the blown up tree root; rested his pistol on a projecting root, took careful aim and as the panther reared up with his forefeet on the log to cross it as he had calculated he would do, Lavesk fired and killed him.

CAPT. JAS. PATTERSON—IMPRISONMENT IN MEXICO

In the Spring of 1809 James Patterson started from Pulaski with three negro men to go to the lead mines in the then Territory of Missouri. After prospecting the mines and perhaps engaging in business a short time, he went to Fort Independence, and from thence in the Fall of the same year with Josiah McClannahan and William Smith, (called Billy Smith), who was a brother of the noted duellist, John Smith, his three negro men, a Spaniard and Indian Interpreter, he set out on horseback for Santa Fe, N. M., with a view of opening up a trade between those places which at that time offered great inducements, to those who should early engage in it. The route was unexplored but knowing the latitude and longitude of the place, he traveled by his compass, as near a direct course as the surface of the country would admit. After many trials and great exposure he reached Santa Fe, with his party at a time when there was some public disturbance, or threatened insurrection, preceding the Revolution for Independence Mr. Patterson and his associates were immediately arrested on the charge of being spies in the interest of the French Government, put in irons and sent under guard to Chihuahua. After arriving at Chihuahua, having had their guns, horses, money, ammunition, etc., taken from them, they were imprisoned and kept heavily ironed for nine months. The irons were then taken off and they were kept in prison nine months longer, during which time they suffered greatly for provisions clothing, and the necessary comforts of life. Capt. Patterson as long as he lived could not talk about his imprisonment without showing in his changed tone of voice and manner, the painful associations which the recurrence brought up. He was a Mason, and the Priest who visited him was also a Mason, and through his influence, as he supposed their condition was rendered more tolerable. At the end of eighteen months they were turned out of prison but not permitted to leave the city, and were required to support themselves as best they could. Smith was a gun-smith and a very ingenious mechanic. He repaired gun-locks, etc., and invented a machine to mill their silver coin in moulding the metal, which he turned to some profit. The Revolution which finally resulted in the independence of Mexico, commenced after they were arrested.

Don Miguel Hidalgo the first leader of the revolution, was captured with others of the insurgents and taken to Chihuahua, whilst Mr. Patterson and his party were there; and was there shot as history shows in July 1811. Mr. Patterson witnessed his execution and in substance thus describes it: Hidalgo requested that he should not be shot in the back, that his eyes should not be bandaged, and that he might be permitted to face his executioners. Two other prisoners were shot at the same time. Four squads of soldiers were detailed to shoot the prisoners. Hidalgo was talking to those around him, told them, "The knell of Spanish rule had sounded." The first squad fired and one of the two prisoners fell. The second squad fired and the other one fell; the third squad fired and Hidalgo was still standing and appeared unmoved and continued to talk to those around as though no danger threatened; with the fourth volley he fell. Colonel Nelson Patterson of this County, (the father of Jas. Patterson) saw in a newspaper an extract from a Vera Cruz paper, published in the City of Mexico, an account of their capture and imprisonment, and wrote to the authorities at Washington. The U. S Government demanded their release from Spain After having been nearly three years prisoners they were permitted to leave, the three negroes and the Indians declined to return with them. The Governor or Commandant of the City gave them back their guns and pistols, and some powder that was so weak they could not kill a deer at more than thirty yards. He also gave them a map by which to travel to reach the United States' at Natchidoches on the Western border of Louisiana. The Governor's Secretary was a Mason, and he told Mr. Patterson privately not to take the route the Governor designated; that the Governor had posted a band of Indians at a certain watering place, on the way where they were to stop, with strict instructions to kill them all; that the Governor did not intend they should reach the U. S. to tell the Americans of the barbarous and inhuman treatment they had received, for fear the United States Government would make a demand on Spain for redress. The Secretary directed them on a different route, which they followed and escaped the Indians.

They set out on foot and traveled through the Southeastern portion of the staked plains, into the Wetsern portion of Texas. They were out of water for three days and in their despair of ever reaching the United States, they decided to separate and each take his own course, and to meet at Natchidoches; and if either lived to get through and the others failed, he was to inform their friends of their imprisonment and that they had perished on the plains. After a great deal of suffering and hardships they all got to Natchidoches. McClannahan first, Patterson two days after, and Smith the next day, without gun, hat, or shoes, and with but little clothing. The Indians had run him for three days through the Chaparell and he barely escaped them. From Natchidoches they came home with but little trouble. Mr. Patterson said they had nothing to eat coming through the plains, except what they killed with their guns; and that the powder had been so prepared and weakened that it was supposed they would not be able to defend themselves against the Indians, or kill any game. They were at one time three days without a bite to eat. Mr. Patterson said that during their sufferings and privations in prison, they had the kind sympathies of the women, who often sent them provisions and other things by stealth. This he always mentioned with feelings of gratitude, and generally with his eyes moistened and subdued voice, and spoke of it as an illustration of the fact that woman has an instinctive sympathy for the oppressed and suffering of her race. Mr. Patterson related several incidents illustrative of the difficulties he had to encounter in traveling over the wild desert; one of which was that he lay one night in a small ravine or gully to protect himself from the North wind. He lay with his gun by him and his pistol in his hand; in the night a wolf came up and smelt of his hand; he could have shot him but the report of the pistol would bring the Indians upon him. He lay with his pistol cocked, pointing at the wolf, resolved to shoot if the wolf made an attack, but the wolf after smelling him, went off without interrupting.

Before Mr. Patterson returned home the war of 1812 had commenced. He went out with the troops under Gen. Jackson in the Fall of 1813, to the Creek Nation and was elected Lieutenant in Captain John Gordon's Company of spies, and had a squad of twenty men put under him for special duty, under the immediate orders of General Jackson.

He carried through the Indian war a large bear gun rife, six feet in length, which carried fourteen balls to the pound. The gun is now in possession of his son, J. Nelson Patterson.

An incident is told of him at the battle of Horse-shoe, which may be worth relating. Mr. Patterson, with his squad was out reconnoitering on one of the flanks of the army. He discovered that a party of Indians were about to cut them off, and believing that the Indians had not seen them ordered his men to fall back to the breastworks. After they started he saw one of his men whose attention was directed another way and did not know of their danger. Being hard of hearing, instead of calling him to attract his attention the doughty soldier ran back to inform him, and they both started for the breastworks. By this time the Indians saw them and pursued them. A tall, athletic, swift-footed, Indian took after Patterson and was close behind, near enough to touch his back a time or two, as he struck at him with his tomahawk, and but for the fact that Patterson wore a thick, buckskin hunting-shirt, he would have probably been killed or wounded. His comrades at the breastworks witnessed the race, with the most intense anxiety; they saw the danger he was in, and hallooed as loud as they could "run, run, run, run." When he got in safe he turned on them with an air of disdain and said using some words not laid down in army regulations, "Did you think I was running jockey?" James Patterson was for many years a prominent and useful citizen of

Gilese County. He contributed liberally of his means to build up schools and to promote the public enterprises of the day. He possessed a good estate, was generous and hospitable. His influence was on the side of law and order, morality and religion. He was born in the State of Virginia, February 29th, 1784, died August 3, 1856.

Lieutenant Kerley and General "Hickory" Jackson—Wm. M. Kerley came to the County in the early part of 1809 with Tyree Rodes and lived a year or two on his farm. He went out with the first troops under the call of the State in the Fall of 1813, for service in the Creek Nation; and was Lieutenant in one of the companies from Giles County. He became somewhat conspicuous by resisting the authority of Gen. Jackson at Fort Deposit, at a time when a portion of the troops were about leaving the army, believing their term of service had expired. I have read no account of the transaction, that is entirely correct according to my information, and none which does justice to Kerley and his comrades.

To fully understand the controversy between General Jackson and his soldiers, it is necessary briefly to recur to the terms of their enlistment. The massacre of Fort Mimms, the thirtieth of August, 1813, startled the whole country and caused a stampede of all the white settlers between Mobile and Huntsville. The Legislature of Tennessee being in session and fearing an immediate advance by the Indians, on her Southern borders, without waiting to consult the general Government, authorized the Governor to call out 3,500 of the militia, in addition to the volunteers who had been discharged in the Spring, after their return from Natchez without limiting their term of service, and pledged the State to pay them if the United States Government refused. The Governor ordered General Jackson to raise two thousand of the number in his division; the balance to be raised in East Tennessee. Under the orders of General Jackson the militia rendezvoused at Huntsville, Oct. 4, 1813, and were mustered into service without specifying the time they were to serve. Near the close of the year General Jackson, learning that the militia expected to be discharged, the fourth of January at the expiration of the three months, insisted that, having been raised under an Act that did not limit their term, and mustered into service without specifying the time they were to serve, by implication they were bound for the shortest time allowed by Act of Congress, which was six months. The officers and soldiers insisted that they were enlisted with the express understanding and belief that it was for a three months campaign; that the militia raised in East Tennessee under the same Act was mustered into service for three months, and were received as such and claimed their discharge the fourth day of January.

General Jackson having received a letter from Governor Blount, indicating his acquiescence in the opinion of the militia, perceived it would be useless to try to hold them; but believing they were bound under the law to serve six months if required, he determined to hold them until reinforcements arrived. Accordingly he issued an order prohibiting them to leave without his permission.

"At half past ten on the morning of the fourth of January, (quoting from Kendall's Life of Jackson), neither the officer of the guard nor any of the sentinels were found at their posts. On the report of this fact General Jackson ordered the arrest of Lieut. Kerley, the officer in question. He refused to surrender his sword, asserting that he was no longer subject to the orders of General Jackson. The General directed Col. Sitler, the Adjutant-General to parade the guards, and Captain Gordon's Company of Spies, and arrest Kerley at all hazards. The order was instantly obeyed. Kerley was found at the head of his Company, which with the rest of the militia was formed and ready to march. Colonel Sitler ordered him to halt but he refused. The Colonel then ordered the guards to stop him, which was done; still he refused to deliver his sword. Sitler then ordered the guards to fire on him if he persisted in his refusal, and both parties simultaneously cocked their guns. At this critical moment Gen. Jackson himself rode up and in person demanded of Kerley the surrender of his sword. Again Kerley refused imperatively. The General drew a pistol from his holster and was levelling it at Kerley's breast when Colonel Sitler placed himself between them, urging him to submit. A friend of Kerley's drew his sword from the scabbard and presented it to Col. Sitler who refused to accept it. Having been returned to Kerley, he finally surrendered it to Col. Sitler and was put under guard."

Charles C. Abernathy of Giles County witnessed the transaction. He says the account given in Kendall's Life of Jackson is substantially correct, except as to Kerley's giving up his sword. He says he had gone to the camp of Dr. Gilbert D. Taylor, then of Pulaski, who was a surgeon in the army; that Col. Sitler stopped Kerley about twenty or thirty yards from Taylor's camp, where he and Dr. Taylor were sitting; that when Kerley refused to surrender his sword "General Jackson, coming up with a pistol in his hand, declared to Kerley, that if he did not give up his sword he would blow him through." At this crisis Dr. Taylor said to me, "This will never do," and immediately left his seat and running to Kerley jerked his sword from his hand, and offered it to Col. Sitler which Sitler refused to receive from him. Dr. Taylor then placed the sword back in Kerley's hand, and taking Kerley's arm with the sword in his hand, extended it to Colonel Sitler, whereupon Col. Sitler received it, and Kerley submitted to arrest." He says, "It is very doubtful whether Kerley would have voluntarily surrendered his sword." That General Jackson certainly would not have parleyed long with him, and that but for the timely interposition of Dr. Taylor, there is no telling what would have been the result; that the opposing forces were nearly equal. He says "During the progress of the affair, I calculated on witnessing the bloodiest time I had ever seen, the result of which would have been the breaking up of the Creek War at least for a season."

After Kerley's arrest he asked pardon of General Jackson, and in explanation of his conduct stated that having promised his company to lead them home, he feared it would be considered a compromise of his courage and his honor to surrender his sword. He was soon released and his sword restored. (It is said that Kerley ordered his men not to fire on the soldiers in case the word was given, but to fire upon Jackson.) He was ever afterwards the friend of General Jackson. The tradition is that General Jackson said Kerley was too brave a man to punish. While the controversy was going on with Kerley, the rest of the Brigade with the exception of Captain Willis and about thirty of his men, marched off and no further effort was made to arrest them.

Dr. Taylor—Having mentioned the name of Dr. Taylor in connection with the arrest of Lieutenant Kerley, it is due to his gallantry, patriotism, and exalted worth, that some record should be made of him. Gilbert D. Taylor was born in Orange County, Virginia, November 18, 1791 in the same house in which his relative, President Taylor, was afterwards born. After pursuing his medical education in Philadelphia, he came to Pulaski in 1811, and commenced the practice of medicine. He soon acquired reputation as a surgeon and for bold and heroic treatment. On the first call for troops for service in the Creek Nation, in the Fall of 1813, he went out under General Jackson, and was appointed surgeon of his regiment. When the term of service of his regiment expired, he was appointed on Gen. Jackson's medical staff, and remained through the Creek campaign. In the battles of Emuckfaw, and Enotochopie, at his own request, he acted with the artillery Company under the command of Lieutenant Armstrong. Not satisfied with his own favorite rifle, which he took from home, he purchased from Major Thomas Wilkinson a smooth bore gun of unusual size and caliber, the barrel of which was five feet long. It carried from thirty-five to forty buckshot at a load. The evening before the expedition left Ft. Strother, he and Chalres C. Abernathy ran a quantity of bullets in his rife moulds which he used as shot in loading, shooting twenty-five rifle balls at a time. At Emuckfaw, when the Indians made an attack before day, Dr. Taylor took good position. He took position by a tree in the dark and watched for the flash of Indian guns and fired at the flash. Whenever he fired, his comrades recognizing the report of the gun, would cry out, "There's Taylor's artillery." An examination of the dead after the battle showed that his big gun had been used to terrible effect.

At the battle of Enotochopie, when Col. Stump and his cavalry became demoralized, by the charge of the Indians in the rear, Dr. Taylor was one of the intrepid twenty-five who defended the ford until the Infantry with the artillery could cross. Of that noble band eighteen were shot down. His coolness and bravery on this occasion called forth the warm comendation of his General. He made a profession of religion in 1814, and in 1819 was ordained a minister of the M. E. Church. He was a faithful and most efficient minister of that Church. He was a man whom all delighted to honor as well those of other creeds, as the members of his own Church. His sympathy with the afflicted, his pastoral visits to the sick, and his affectionate interest in their spiritual welfare, knew no bounds, and greatly endeared him to all. He died the sixth of August, 1870, in the 79th year of his age. "The Memory of the Righteous is Blessed."

MARTIN, BALLENTINE AND CARTER

A record of Giles County would be incomplete without a memorial of three of her citizens who came some years after the first settlers but who for nearly forty years filled a large place in her history; who, by their energy perseverance, integrity, liberality and enlarged views of public policy, left their impression for good on the present generation. I refer to Thomas Martin, A. M. Ballentine and Dr. Ben Carter. No men ever enjoyed more fully the confidence of the community in which they lived, and none ever more deserved it. They were leaders in their day in all the public enterprises in the County. As prominent and successful merchants, they exercised a large and controlling influence on the mercantile interests of the County. So much so, that for twenty years before the war, there was only one or two mercantile failures in Pulaski, and but very few in the County.

Thomas Martin was born in Albemarle, County, Virginia, December 16th, 1799, moved from Sumner County to Giles County in 1818, was married to Miss Nancy Topp, Oct. 12th, 1824, and died in Pulaski, January 13th, 1870.

Andrew M. Ballentine was born in Tyrone County, Ireland, in 1791, and under a provision of the laws of the country at that time, he served seven years in the British army. At the expiration of his term he migrated to the United States, and landed at Philadelphia, where he remained for several years in a wholesale dry goods house at very small wages, until an offer was made to him by George Crockett, of Nashville. Having no money to pay traveling expenses, they were paid by Crockett, and he lived with Crockett as a clerk for some time, until he paid the debt and came to Giles County in 1815, and settled on Robertson's Fork at the Jones' place, now known as the Fitzpatrick place, where he established a small store, and married the daughter of John Goff. He moved to Pulaski in 1821, where he resided until his death, June 27th, 1863, at the age of seventy-two.

Dr. Benjamin Carter was born in Sumpter County, S. C., June the 14th, 1792. He moved with his father at an early date to Maury County, Tennessee. Having read medicine and attended lectures in Philadelphia, he settled at Elkton about 1817, and practiced medicine there for many years. He was married June 13th, 1822, to Elizabeth K. Lindsay. About 1829 he moved to Pulaski; practiced a year or two, and then engaged in the mercantile business. He died the 16th day of July, 1865. These men had no distinguished lineage to boast of, nor the armorials of noble ancestry; but they had what was more valuable, they were endowed by nature with a large share of common sense; they were men of untiring industry, energy and perseverance, and consistently just in all their dealings. And besides they were Christian gentlemen, whose influence and liberality in their respective churches, were exercise for great good. They have left an example worthy of imitation by the youth of our country, which, if followed will lead to success.

MASONIC LODGES

The first Masonic Lodge established in Giles County was Laurence Lodge, No. 16, at Pulaski, instituted by dispensation issued August the 4th, 1816, by Robert Searcy, Gr. M., but it is not known who were the charter members. But from a roll of the members certified to by Amos Davis, Sec'y., the names of those who were members in January 1818, were given. As it may be interesting to some of their descendants I will give their names here to-wit: Shadrak Nye, W. M., James Patterson, S. W., Thomas B. Jones, J. W., Henry Hagan, Treasurer, Amos Davis, Secretary, T. B. Haynie, S. D. J. S. Connor, J. D., William Hamby, St., William R. Davis, Tyler, David Reed, Samuel Cooper, A. Rogers, J. M. Phillips, S. Y. Anderson, William Kelly, N. Patterson, N. Davis, G. H. Edwards, Lewis Connor, A. M. Harris, J. B. Connor, M. C. Mc-Cormack, B. M. Patterson, Tryon M. Yancey, G. Kearney, Jas. Frazier, Enoch Davis, T. Williams, J. D. Graves, F. Hicks, Harrison Hicks, Thomas Smith, James Perry and John Samuel.

In 1821 the lodge failed to elect officers, at the time required and ceased to work for more than two years, by which the Charter was forfeited. In October 1824 a charter was granted for a new Lodge by the name of LaFayette Lodge No. 51, to Thos. B. Jones, W. M., Alf M. Harris, S. W., Alex S. Jones, J. W., and others. At the annual meeting of the Grand Lodge in 1825, Aaron V. Brown, William C. Flournoy and V. Loring were delegates, at which communication A. V. Brown was elected Junior Warden. The Lodge was prosperous for many years. Among the prominent members not named were Dr. Alf Flournoy, Dr. Gilbert D. Taylor, Dr. Chas. Perkins, Dr. L. Cooper, Dr. Elisha Eldridge, Dr. E. R. Field, Sterling H. Lester, John K. Yerger, Collin S. Tarpley, Spencer Clack, L. H. Brown and others. During the suspension of Masonry from about 1834 to about 1841, the Lodge ceased to work and the records and jewels were were lost. In 1842 on petition of William H. Field, James McCallum, Samuel J. Rogers and others, a dispensation was issued by Frand Master Tannehill for a new Lodge called Pulaski Lodge, No. 101, which was chatered in due time and is still in existence.

The second Lodge in the County was Elkton Lodge No. 24, at Elkton, instituted under dispensation issued November 28th, 1818, by Gr. M. Wilkins Tannehill. The early records have been lost and it is not known who were the charter members; but at two meetings of the Grand Lodge in 1819, Dr. Ben Carter was delegate to one, and Dr. John H. Camp to the other. Among the early members were: Dr. Jno. H. Camp, James Camp, Ben Carter, Gustin Kearney, Robert B. Harney, William Phillips, Thos. Phillips, John Hawkins, Wyth Sims, Wm. H. Moore, Wm. S. Neal, Matthew Black and Abel Wilson.

The Lodge having made no returns from 1822 to 1827, and having ceased to work, in 1827 a number of members applied for authority to form themselves into a Lodge. The

Grand Master advised them to do so under the old Charter, which was declared irregular at a meeting of the Grand Lodge, and a new Charter granted with the name and number of the old Lodge with Archer Phillips, W. M., A. M. Upshaw, S. W., and Thomas Phillips, J. W. Among the prominent members a few years later, in addition to some of those already named were Dr. Dabney B. Phillips, Dr. Zeno T. Harris, Dr. William E. Harold, Dr. W. H. Butler, Pinckney B. Wilson, Hardy Benson Claiborne Kyle, Henry and William Jones, P. H. Braden, William Braden, James McCallum, George D. Scruggs, Charles Leatherman, David J. Moore, Wm. Monroe and others.

During the general suspension from 1834 to 1841, Elkton Lodge did not surrender her Charter, or abandon her organization, but met occasionally without doing any regular work, except to bury the dead, etc. In the Fall of 1842 the Lodge with the permission of the Grand Master resumed work and is still in existence.

The Lodges in Pulaski and Elkton were the only ones in the County, previous to 1845. Since that date Lodges have been established at Cornersville, Bethel, Lynnville, Bradshaw, (since removed to Pisgah), Campbellsville, Prospect and Bodenham.

A number of Lodges of I. O. O. F. were established in the County before the war, but members of the order requested to furnish statistics have failed to do so.

CONCLUSION

It is said to be an axiom that no people ever lose their prosperity, but by departing from the principles to which they owed their success. In looking back to the early settlers of our County, what were the principles that actuated them— what was the dominant idea that advanced their national prosperity? It was to purchase nothing they could produce, or make themselves, to sell more than they bought, and to live within their income, be it much or little.

In conclusion it is impossible to contemplate the early settlement of our County, in its varied scenes, without admiration for the character of its early settlers. Their constant exercise of body, and mode of life invigorated their constitutions, and fitted them to endure hardship and fatigue. Their necessities stimulated their inventive genius, and developed their mental powers; their isolated condition and exposure to danger, made them self-reliant and courageous. They often courted danger "for danger's sake." Their intercourse with each other was most cordial and friendly, they called each other by their Christian names. There was then no rival grades or social distinctions in their respective neighborhoods, but all who were honest, honorable and industrious stood on a par. Enterprise and courage gave to each a knowledge of his own capacity, while friendship, confidence, and mutual dependence, knit them together as a band of brothers. Cherished be their memories, green be the sod that covers their neglected graves.

PART SECOND—DESCRIPTION OF THE COUNTY

The boundaries of Giles County as defined by the Legislature, commenced at the S. E. corner of Maury County; thence S. to the S. boundary, of the State; thence W. far enough to include a constitutional County; (625 square miles) thence N. to the Maury County line; thence E. to the Maury County line to the beginning. The width of the County from East to West is about —— miles. The Northern boundary follows the meanders of the ridge that divides the waters of Duck River from those of the Elk. As originally established the Eastern boundary from North to South was about —— miles. At the middle of the County about —— miles, further West about —— miles, averaging about —— or —— miles, making the area slightly over six hundred and twenty-five square miles.

Since the late war a portion of the North-eastern part of the county embracing Cornersville, containing about —— or —— squaure miles, was cut off and added to Marshall County, leaving the County with about —— square miles. No county in Middle Tennessee is better watered than Giles—both as to springs and running streams.

Lynn Creek rises in the Northern part of the County, flows South into Robertson Fork, one and a half miles below Old Lynnville.

Robertson Fork rises in the North-eastern part of the County, flows a South-western direction, until it passes the middle of the County. Then it turns South and enters Richland Creek, a mile or two below Reynolds Station.

Richland Creek, so appropriately named by General Rob- about three miles South of the original North-east corner of the County, flows an irregular south-western direction, until it passes the middle of the County, thence South a few miles, and then turns to the West, forming a large curve, going three or four miles West of the middle of the County, receiving on its curve to the West, first Big Creek, which rises in the North-western part of the County; next Dry Creek and then Weakley's Creek, which with its tributaries rises in the West and North-western part of the County. Below Weakley it curves to the East and again comes to the middle of the County at Pulaski, having received Moore's Creek on the right hand side. Above Pulaski after passing Buford Station, it receives on the East Haywood's Creek and Pigeon Roost Creek. From Pulaski its general direction is South-east, flowing into Elk River about five miles East of the middle of the County. It receives no streams of importance below Pulaski from the West. On the East side some distance below Pulaski, it receives Buchanan Creek, Newton's Creek and Silver Creek. On the East boundary of the County is Bradshaw's Creek which flows South into Elk River. Between Bradshaw and Buchanan's Creek is Indian Creek, which flows South into Elk River.

Elk River enters the Eastern boundary of the County six miles North of the South-east corner of the County, and flows an irregular South-western direction, passing out about the middle of the Southern boundary.

The South-western part of the County is watered by Ford's Creek, Jenkin's Creek, Shoal and Sugar Creeks, with their tributaries, all flowing South and South-east into Elk River. The lands on Richland Creek from its source to its mouth, are among the best and most productive lands in Middle Tennessee. The broad valley of tillable land on Richland from its entrance on the Eastern boundary with those of its tributaries to the mouth of Weakley, and up Weakley and its tributaries to the Western boundary of the County, presents a broad scope of country across the County of unsurpassed beauty and fertility.

From Pulaski East and North-east is a chain of hills and highlands which divide the waters which flow North into Richland, from those flowing South into Bradshaw, Indian Creek and Buchanan Creek. The lands on these creeks as well as those on Newton's Creek and Silver Crek, are all of the same quality as those on Richland, but not in as large bodies. The lands on both sides of Elk River, generally for some distance lie well, and are regarded as the best cotton lands in the County. From Pulaski on a South-western direction, an irregular chain of hills and highlands, separates the waters which flow North into Weakley and Richland above Pulaski, from those which flow South into Ford's Creek, Jenkin's Creek, Shoal and Sugar Creeks. The valleys on these creeks are very rich and productive, but not in as large bodies generally as are on Richland above Pulaski.

The numerous streams and valleys of the County are separated by hills and highlands, rising sometimes four or five hundred feet above the water level. The most of these hills especially those on Richland, and its upper tributaries, and those between Bradshaw and Richland, are especially productive, even where they are too steep for cultivation. Blue grass grows well upon most of the hillsides. The lands in the Eastern and North-eastern part of the County and the adjoining lands in Lincoln and Marshall, are as fine lands for blue grass as any in the State. There is a grass lot a mile or two from Cornersville in Marshall County, that was sown over sixty years ago, and has been a grass lot ever since, and affords good grazing now, as I learned recently from Colonel McClelland, who owns the place. I mention this place because I recollect no other that has stood so long without being cultivated. There was a large grass lot on the old Robert Gordone farm, sown about the same time which was a good grass lot at the time the old man died, and for several years after. It was grazed for more than thirty years, and some of it may yet be in a grass lot, but a portion has been cultivated since his death. The original forest growth when the early settlers came, was unsurpassed in grandeur and beauty. To one who never saw it till felled by the axe of the hardy pioneer, it is hardly possible to describe it. It abounded in the principle species of trees that are found in other counties in Middle Tennessee, but the markd difference was in their size and massive dimensions. This was noticeably so on Richland and its upper tributaries, and between Richland and Brandshaw. The poplar, beech, sugar tree, elm, walnut, lynn, oak, scaly-bark, (hickory), and white oak were larger than I ever saw any where else, except in the portions of Lincoln and Marshall, lying contiguous, and being of similar quality of soil and timber from five to seven feet in diameter. White oak from five to six feet, beech, black walnut, ash, scaly-bark, hickory, sugar tree, elm and lynn were four or five feet in diameter. Their sizes were not unusually large for Giles County—occasionally some were found larger than these. Grape vines were numerous and very large. The timbers were unusually large where Pulaski is situated and particularly on what is now the public square and along First and Second Main Streets. I remember where there was a grove of the largest size beech trees North-west of where the Methodist Church stands and West of G. W. Woodring's residence I have heard the old settlers speak of a very large poplar that stood on or near the public square that was between five and six feet in diameter. It was blown down soon after the first settlers came. Two or three paths through the cane to the spring passed by it and it was a place of resort for some time for afternoon gatherings, and for those who amused themselves playing cards. A remarkable feature in the forest growth was noticeable in the difference in the growth of the East and West side of Richland below Pulaski and for a few miles above. Whilst the timber on the East side of the creek was of the largest size of poplar, beech, white oak, sugar tree, elm, etc., that on the West side was of a smaller scale in size, embracing most of the varieties on the East side, but abounding more in white oak, hickory and poplar of a smaller size. The soil on the West side is different from that on the East, but not the less productive. For wheat and some other crops it is said to have some advantages. The most remarkable feature in the scenery of the County was the dense cane brakes, which covered the greater portion of the country. On the creek bottoms and on the rich, black soil the cane was from 10 to 16 feet in height. On the rich poplar and beech uplands, it was from eight to twelve feet, and on the ridges and thin land from five to eight feet. The latter was called maiden cane. On some of the poor ridges and those of the character of barrens there was little cane, and where there was no cane the ground was covered with a wild pea vine. To stand on a high hill or knob at the head of a long valley of cane brake, after a light shower of rain, with the sun shining brightly and with a breeze sufficient to keep the tops of the cane and leaves in gentle motion, is one of the grandest sights mortal ever beheld. At that time there was but little undergrowth of timber; no bushes or thickets of bushes as we now have. The forest trees generally had long clean bodies, much freer from limbs near the ground, than at the present day. This of course added greatly to the beauty and grandeur of the scenery.

.One of the difficulties encountered by the first settlers in opening roads through the large cane, was that it was necessary to cut the cane below the surface of the ground, otherwise the stubs of the cane were almost as dangerous to men and beast as if they were steel spikes, and numerous were the accidents to man and beast from cane cut above the ground. For several years after the first settlers came horses and cattle from the more Northern counties were driven into the county for the benefit of the range. This sometimes gave rise to serious complaints by the settlers. It was alleged that those who drove off the foreign stock, some times took more than they brought. This was particularly the case during the war of 1812 when the demand was great for horses and beef cattle. Unprincipled men gathering stock for army contractors, frequently took out more than they purchased. Besides the proximity to Indian territory and the want of organized courts, for a few years, afforded bad men opportunity often to take off stock with impunity.

The fertility of the soil in those dense cane brakes for a few years after the cane was removed was remarkable. The mold which had accumulated for ages from the decaying leaves was so deep and loose that a walking stick could be easily thrust into the ground a foot and often half its length. After the removal of the cane but little labor was required to raise corn, besides cutting down the cane sprouts. The large yield of corn and the little labor required to cultivate it, soon made corn abundant and cheap. Five grains were usually planted in a hill, all matured and made good corn. Five stalks were grown there as well or better than three in the adjoining land of same quality, cleared twenty years after the cane was gone. In a few years after the cane became tramped by stock, the cane began to fail. It showed it first in the large cane on the rich lands. When it began to fail it died out very fast. The small cane on the ridges and thin land lasted several years longer than the large cane. The vitality of the cane root is wonderful. Land in the immediate vicinity of Pulaski that has been cleared and enclosed for sixty years, and cultivated a portion of the time when left uncultivated a few years, if the stock is kept off it, grows up in cane and would soon make cane thickets if undisturbed. One of the peculiarities in the cane is that it acquires its growth in height and size the first year. Some of the largest and tallest cane I ever saw was the first year's growth. They can be easily told; not only by their appearance, but by being soft and easily cut with a knife; the outer surface or enamel does not harden the first year, and in this way they are distinguished from the old cane although of the same size.

Memory recalls no incident in my early life more vividly than one associated with the cane brakes. When a boy my father ranged his cattle two or three miles from home. He salted them every week. I frequently went out with him. The place of salting was on the top of a high ridge, with a valley of cane brake on each side. The cane on one side was a mile or two in extent. The cattle were accustomed to the call of my father. To stand on the top of the hill when the weather was favorable, etc., and look down the valley on either side, and see the cane tops waving to the breeze, hear the sleek cattle responding to the call and witness their rush to get to the salt through the cane was highly exciting.

WURTEMBURG ACADEMY

On the 23rd of November, 1809, nine days after the county was established, the Legislature chartered an Academy for Giles County, called Pulaski Academy, and appointed as Trustees thereof, John Sappington, Nelson Patterson, Tyree Rodes, Samuel Jones, Somerset Moore, Charles Buford, and Charles Neely. In September, 1812, the name of the Academy was changed to Wurtemburg Academy, and Dr. William Purnell, David Woods and Alfred M. Harris, appointed additional Trustees. There being a surplus fund, the proceeds of the sale of the town lots in the hands of the Commissioners of the town of Pulaski, after paying for the public buildings, etc., on application to the Legislature they were authorized to invest a portion of it in a purchase of the large lot on which the Wurtemburg Academy building was erected. For a number of years the Legislature exercised the right to appoint trustees for the Academy. The Academy was well attended and the teachers generally men of solid attainments, and with a great deal of practical common sense. Their discipline was rigid and exacting, and one of the results was that our Academy soon had the reputation of being an admirable school in which to prepare young men to enter college.

I have not access to any records which would enable me to give the names of the different teachers, in this time honored institution, with the order in which they taught. Suffice it to state from my own recollection, that about 1824, the Academy was for several years under the direction of the late William W. Potter, who was a very efficient teacher, and disciplinarian. About 1826 or 1827, a Mr. Loring from Bowling Green, Ky., was at the head of the Institution, for some time; and was very successful in sustaining its reputation. He afterwards became eminent in Kentucky as a lawyer and Judge, and was a most estimable Christian gentleman. About 1834 a Mr. Price had charge of the school. He afterwards acquired reputation as a lawyer and judge in Mississippi. About 1841 or 1842 Mr. Mendum was at the head of the institution some time. He ha d aconsiderable reputation as an instructor and disciplinarian. About 1846 or 1847 John C. Brown (then just returned from college, and since Governor and Confederate General), with Daniel, G. Anderson had charge of the shool one or two sessions. Brown exhibited remarkable talent as an instructor and evinced thorough knowledge of books. After them Benjamin F. Mitchell and John A. Mc-Roberts had charge of the school a number of years. Mr. Mitchell had the reputation of being a ripe scholar and a successful teacher. Mc Roberts was peculiarly adapted to imparting instruction to youth, and had considerable reputation as a teacher. Mr. Mitchell married a daughter of Edward D. Jones, Esq., in the neighborhood and left the Academy and entered the practice of law. Woodbury Mitchell with James L. Jones had charge of the school a session or two I believe, and were successful as teachers. Mr. Mitchell is now the able and popular pastor of Zion Church in Maury County, and Mr. Jones is at present the Chairman of our County Court. In 1849 a college charter was obtained for the old Academy by the name of Giles College, and suitable buildings erected, etc. Prof. Sharpe, Prof. Jno. H. Stewart and Prof. Chas. G. Rogers, were successively in charge, of the College, associated with them most of the time was McRoberts and Alfred H. Abernathy. Stewart had the reputation of being a profound scholar. Rogers as a teacher of mathematics had few superiors. Abernathy and McRoberts were long connected with the school and were eminently successful. During the late war our college buildings were used as a Federal hospital, and were so much damaged during the war that the principle building had in a great measure to be rebuilt, the loss of which, with other liabilities required the college property to be sold.

FEMALE ACADEMY

At a very early date a first-class female school was established under the name of the "Female Academy." The first building erected or obtained for the Academy, was on the lot now owned by J. B. Childers, and on which he has long reisded. Without attempting to enumerate the teachers, I will mention a few who were personally known to me. The years 1827 or 1828, the Rev. James Hall Brooks took charge of the Academy, and taught several years. He was a superior teacher and disciplinarian. Under his managment the patronage of the Academy increased, and made considerable reputation. A few years later the first Academy buildings were sold or exchanged for the lot on which the Episcopal Rectory is now situated. This site was more central to the patrons of the school. After the school was opened in the new buildings it was under the management successively of Mr. Thomason, an Englishman, Mr. Davis, Dr. Rawles, and others. In 1842 or 1843, the Reverend Robert Caldwell took charge of it, and continued the management with competent assistants for a number of years, until 1853 or 1854 or perhaps later, when the condition of the building from a crack in the wall, or other cause, was deemed unsafe and not worthy of having necessary improvements made to it; and the lot and building was sold a short time before the late war. Our "Female Academy" unpretentious as it was, had the reputation of sending girls and young ladies to higher schools, better drilled and more thoroughly taught in what they professed to have studied, than from almost any other place.

COTTON MILLS

About 1847 or 1848 a charter was obtained for a manufacturing company, and the name of the "Richland Manufacturing Company," at Pulaski, under which a company was soon organized. Buildings were erected and "Pulaski Cotton Mills" started about 1850. They have been in successful operation for most of the time since, and but for the late war would doubtless have been a valuable investment for the stockholders.

RAILROAD

In 1856 the County subscribed $275,000. payable in five annual installments, to build the section of the present Nashville and Decatur railroad from Columbia to the Alabama line. The road was completed in 1860, or about that date. Although the road has fullfilled perhaps the expectations of the general public, in facilities for transportation and travel, yet, strange to say, our citizens have become more indifferent to building turn-pikes and keeping up the country roads, than they were before we had the railroad. This doubtless may be attributed in part to our system of labor and our County producing little else for market besides cotton.

COURT HOUSE AND JAIL

The first Court held in the County was a Court of Pleas and Quarter Sessions on the third Monday in February, 1810, at the house of Lewis Kirk, who lived in a log cabin on the bank of Richland Creek, at the foot of the shoals about 200 yards above the Nashville and Decatur depot. The Court was held in a rough house, erected in Kirk's yard for that purpose, and was called the first Court House.

About the same time a rough log cabin was erected near it for a jail, and this was called the first jail. Persons were imprisoned in it for misdemeanors, contempt of Court, etc. Those charged with felonies, etc., were for the first two or three years sent to the Williamson County jail, after that for two or three years to Maury County jail. The tradition is that while the jail at Kirk's was used, a good fiddler was imprisoned for some minor offense, and occasionally a party in town who were fond of amusement (some of them men of influence and high standing) would go to the jail in the night after bedtime, prize up one corner of the house, block it up, take out the prisoner, carry him up into town, fiddle and frolic until nearly day, then take him back put him in prison and let down the corner of the house again. After the sale of lots in August, 1811, the cane having been cut down on the public square, a court house was built on the public square about where the gate of the present court yard fence it. It was built out of round logs, covered with boards, in which courts were held about two years. The first Circuit Court held in it was December 1811. The records of the Court show that the Court was opened on the first day of the term, at the house of Lewis Kirk, and adjourned to meet at the Court House. This was called the second Court House. About the same time a log house was built for a jail, near the South-east corner of the public square, and near the South-west corner of the drug store lately occupied by Pope & Gordon. The Commissioners of the town were required by Act of the Legislature, after paying for the land on which the town was located from a sale of the lots, to use enough of the proceeds of the sale of the lots to build a Court House, jail and stocks. The Commissioners although they had ample funds, delayed erecting the public buildings until the citizens

became impatient, and the Court House was burned one night
Tradition says it was burnd with the assent and full knowledge of some of the most influential citizens, to force the
Commissioners to build a suitable house. Whether the citizens instigated the burning or not, they did not regret it.
When the house was burning some of those present were
active in bringing out the benches, and trying to save as
much as they could. Whilst others, and most of them men of
influence, were as active in throwing them back. When one
of them, a prominent citizen was asked why he was throwing
the benches and tables back, he said he was "trying to
smother the damned fire."

The minutes of the Circuit Court at April term, 1814,
show rather a singular entry in relation to the burning to-
wit: At a Circuit Court began and held for the county of Giles
on Monday the 20th day of April, 1814, on the place where
the Court House lately stood, in the town of Pulaski, present
the Honorable Thos. Stewart, Judge, etc. "The Court House
being burnt, it is therefore ordered that Court be adjourned
to meet at the house of Daniel Martin immediately."

The Court was held that term at the house of Daniel Martin, (the father of our David S. Martin.) At the April term
1815 Court was held at the house of Isaac Smith, in the town
of Pulaski. He was a brother of the late Samuel S. Smith, and
Capt. Tom Smith (Tub Smith.) About the time the Court
House was burned or soon after, a citizen from the country
of some property and influence but at times boisterous, was
sent to jail for contempt of court. He was greatly enraged at
having to go to jail and especially at having to be locked up
in a log pen, where those passing could see him through the
cracks; and he swore that no other person should be so hu-
miliated. That night the jail was burned, whether by him or
some other person no one seemed to care. It is evident the
citizens were rather pleased that it was burnd.

The Commissioners of the town soon contracted with
Archibald Alexander, a citizen of the place, to build a Court
House, and with Phillip P. Maury of Williamson County to
build a jail. A substantial two-story brick Court House was
erected, by Alexander on the site of the present Court House
It was considered a fine Court House at that day. It stood a

long time, when it was taken down and another Court House
was built on the same site, of larger dimensions and on a different plan. This was a large, fine looking house. In a year
or two after it was erected it accidentally took fire in the
cornice, from a defective flue in the wall and was burned
down.

Courts were then held for a year or two in the old Odd
Fellows Hall on the first floor. In a few years after the burning the present Court House was built, which is one of the
best built houses in the State, and in point of symmetrical
proportions it is not surpassed by any building I ever saw.
The late Colonel Heiman of Nashville was the architect who
furnished the plan and directed the erection of the building.
To insure good walls the Commissioners contracted for the
brick to be delivered and counted, in the Court House yard,
all to be hard brick. and whole brick.   They   procured
other materials, hired the best brick masons by the day and
employed the late F. H. Wilkerson who was a mechanic himself of large experience to superintend the work.   The late
George W. Tillery executed the wood work. This may be said
to be the fifth Court House we have had, two of wood and
three of brick.   The present Court House is still an excellent
house.

The jail contracted to be built by Maury in 1814, was
erected on the North-west corner of the public square where
the jail long stood. When the building was completed, want-
ing only one or two hour's work, it was accidentally burned,
it is said by shavings taking fire from some persons who had
gone into the house at night to play cards.   The building
would probably have been received by the Commissioners
the next day, but as it had not been reecived, held that the
loss must fall on the contractor that they were acting under
the authority of the Legislature, and had no discretion; that
the funds were from the sale of the town lots which they
would have to account for, and accordingly sued Maury for
$2400. advanced on the contract, and   recovered   judgment
against him in the Circuit Couht of Williamson County. On
petition to the Legislature by a number of citizens of Giles,
John Bell, who was then a member of the Legislature, from
Wililamson County, procured the passage of a bill relieving

Maury from the payment of said judgment and making the payment of the $2400. to him by the Commissioners a valid credit to them on final settlement, and also authorizing them to pay him six hundred dollars more, being half the balance due on the contract, provided the County Court should be of opinion that such payment would be just and equitable under the circumstances; and make an order on their minutes to that effect, a copy of which order should authorize the Commissioners to pay over the money. Another jail was soon erected on the same site, by, I think, the same contractor, which was in its way a good, safe jail—and remained until near the close of the late war, when it was burned down it is said by the retreating Confederate Army. It had been used by the Federal authorities to imprison citizens when arrested, and it is said was in a very foul and loathsome condition, and was burned to keep our citizens when arrested from being imprisoned in so unhealthy and loathsome a place. Afterward the County Court decided to remove the jail from the public square, and had the present neat and excellent jail erected, on First Main Street; the lot on which the old jail stood being sold for a very fair price. Our present jail is the fifth one erected in the county, two of which were log houses and three of brick.

JUDGES OF THE CIRCUIT COURT

Thos. Stewart was the first Judge of our Circuit Court. He was elected Judge of the Fourth Judicial Circuit, which embraces Giles County, at the same session the Legislature adopted the Circuit Court system, in place of the old Superior Courts. He resided in Williamson County near Franklin. He had the reputation of being an able judge and a man of unimpeachable integrity. As illustrative of the man and of the times, I beg leave to give an incident in Judge Stewart's life, told me by Mr. John Goff, long a citizen of this county. Before he came to this County he was a near neighbor of Judge Stewart. In harvest time Mr. Goff had a reaping to which all his neighbors were invited. Wheat and other small grain at that day was cut with the old-fashioned sickle. Every neighbor carried with him his own sickle. As in the days of the Patriarchs reaping was not only a time of substantial help to neighbors, but they were times of feasting and social enjoyment. Judge Stewart was quite an old man, occupying the position of Judge and was invited, not to labor—but to participate in the entertainment and the social enjoyment of the day. The Judge came on the day appointed with his sickle. Mr. Goff explained to him that he did not expect him to engage in the harvest field. The Judge said he had come to the reaping and would take part with the reapers. Mr. Goff was a man of fine size and of unusual physical powers, led an active life and was a good reaper, as he thought. After the other reapers got well on their way, Mr. Goff and the Judge sat it. Mr. Goff said he dashed off rapidly and thought to leave the Judge immediately, but to his surprise he found that the Judge kept close up to him. He then let himself out at his best speed thinking to tire the Judge, as the round they were cutting was of considerable length, still the Judge kept up. Goff said he very soon found out that, instead of running away from the Judge, it was necessary to exert his full physcial powers to keep up with him, and by the time he got around he was willing to rest himself, while the Judge was apparently not fatigued. To those who never witnessed an old-fashioned reaping, it is difficult for them to appreciate the excitement.

The Legislature of 1817, established the Sixth Judicial Circuit, composed of the counties of Maury, Lincoln, Bedford, Giles and Lawrence. Alfred M. Harris of Pulaski was elected Judge of the New Circuit. He was an earnest, forcible, speaker and an able advocate. He improved the place on the hill West of the Public Suare. The same on which the Esq. E. W. Rose resided at the time of his death. His law office was on the South-east corner of his lot, two or three hundred yards from the public square. When asked why he did not have his office nearer the Court House, he said, men who had important suits, and were able to pay good fees, would find him readily enough. He resigned in the Fall of 1821.

Robert Mack of Columbia succeeded him, first by the appointment of the Governor, afterwards by the election of the Legislature, the 26th of September, 1821. He was a man of strong native intellect, of great industry and perseverance, and with some eccentricities. He labored under many disadvantages in coming to the bar, as many other young men at that day did, who afterwards became prominent in the State; he attended the first courts held in our County soon after he was licensed. An incident occurred at the first Court he attended, which was the first or second Circuit Court held in the County, that I will here relate. At that time there were but few houses in the town and Colonel Nelson Patterson who was a hospitable old Virginia gentleman living half a mile from town, invited Colonel Thos. H. Benton, Mr. Mack and two or three other lawyers to his house. They all occupied the same room, when preparing to retire for the night, Mack requested the boy that waited on him to bring in a needle and thread in the morning, stating that he wanted to "fix his gallows" (meaning his suspenders,) Benton made some playful remark about it, and in the morning when the boy came in, Benton asked him if he had brought the needle and thread, which he had not; when he came in the second time, Benton asked the question again; jocularly remarking that he wanted Mack to "fix his gallows" Mack felt keenly the reflection, and retorted with some warmth, "Now Bent, don't trouble yourself about my "gallows,"—if you keep on as you've started the government will some day fix your gallows." Benton took it all in good humor. The effect was that none of them ever afterwards attempted to have sport at Mack's expense. Judge Mack resigned in 1826.

William E. Kennedy, then of Fayetteville, succeeded him, first by appointment of the governor, and then by election of a call session in 1826. At the time he accepted the appointment he was the Representative in the Senate from Giles and Lincoln; and Aaron V. Brown was elected in his place for the call session of the Legislature. Judge Kennedy was an able fearless, and upright Judge; a man of great firmness and dignity of character. Without ostentation or show of authority, he maintained the dignity of the Court more completely than any Judge I ever saw on the Bench. There was a magnetism or something about the man—his manner or look—that impressed all who attended Court; without the difference between familiarity off the Bench, and what was due to the dignity of the Court when in session. He was a devoted friend. An incident occurred in one of his last courts, which in justice to his memory, and as an example to the rising generation, should be recorded. At one of his courts in an adjoining county a poor, worthless, drunken man was indicted on a charge of petit larceny, I believe; when the case was called the Judge told the Attorney General that he could not try the case; that as worthless as the man was they were in the army together, (the war of 1812) in the same mess or company, that while in the army, the man had befriended him or done him a favor—under circumstances he could never forget, and if the trial was pressed as he was not legally incompetent to try it—he would resign. But told the Attorney General that if he would continue the case he would have some other Judge to hold the next term of Court. Before the next term Judge Kennedy resigned attended the next term and defended the poor man as a lawyer, and with his able argument and persuasion cleared him. Knowing both men as I did, I regard this as the highest exhibition of undying gratitude I ever knew. Such a man never forsakes a friend if he should be unfortunate and lose his popularity and influence as too many of the present day do. Judge Kennedy resigned in the Summer of 1833.

Lunsford M. Bramlette, of Pulaski, succeeded him, first by appointment of the Governor, and then by election of the Legislature, Oct. 7th, 1833. He held the office until the early part of the year 1836, when he went on the Bench as Chancellor.

Edmund Dillihunty succeeded Judge Bramlette early in 1836; having been elected by the Legislature in the Fall of 1835. He was an able and faithful Judge, and was deservedly popular with the people. His large influence was persistently exerted in behalf of the people, for education, temperance, morality and religion. Our State can boast of but few such Judges as Dillihunty and Kennedy. He continued in office until his death in January or first of February, 1852. William P. Martin succeeded him, first by appointment from the Governor then by election by the Legislature in the Fall of 1853. Soon after by election by the people, the fourth Thursday of May 1854, the Constitution having been amended so as to give the election of Judges and Attorney Generals to the people.

Nature was bountiful in her gifts to Judge Martin. Besides being endowed with a strong and vigorous intellect, ready perception and fine imagination, he had a wonderful flow of spirits, and was genial and social in a high degree. He was long a member of the Presbyterian Church, and was a faithful and conscientious Judge. He held the office until the courts were closed by the late war. He was re-elected by the people in 1870, under the provisions of the new Con stitution, and held the office at the time of his death.

CHANCELLORS

The first Chancery Court held in Pulaski under the separate Chancery system, was by the Honorable W. A. Cook, Chancellor, etc., in April 1832.

Lunsford M. Bramlette was elected Chancellor by the Legislature in the Fall of 1835, under the provisions of the Constitution of 1834, and entered upon the duties of his office in the early part of 1836. He held the office eight years until the Spring of 1844. Judge Bramlette was born in Surrey County, N. C., brought up in Wilkes County, Ga., came to Tennessee in 1813, and was admitted an attorney in the courts of this County in April, 1814. Possessed of a good mind, strict integrity, and great energy of purpose, by close application to his profession he succeeded in a few years in getting an extensive and lucrative practice, which he retained until he went on the Bench in 1833. He was a good lawyer and a good advocate, but as a speaker he was neither eloquent nor graceful; but withal he was forcible, earnest and sincere. He seldom had an important case on hand long that he did not enter into the feelings of his client, and believed he was right; and whether he gained the case or not, he generally succeeded in gaining the lasting good will of his client.

Mr. Grundy took advantage of this weakness of Judge Bramlette on one occasion, when he was opposing counsel. The character of Bramlette's client was not the best and Grundy abused him most unmercifully, from the very start, and kept Bramlette so irritated and excited that he did not make out his case as strong as he might have made it, and

Grundy gained the case, when it was said the merits of the case were against him. As a Chancellor he was slow in forming his opinions, but generally correct. He had an exalted opinion of the law. After he retired from practice, nothing more interested him than to listen to a good legal argument. If a question was raised about which he was not satisfied, he would look up the authorities with as much care and interest as if he were interested. He was a courteous, dignified lawyer, of the old school, conscientiously just and upright. He was for many years an elder and prominent member of the Presbyterian Church in Pulaski. He died at an advanced age.

Terry H. Cahal, of Columbia, succeeded Judge Bramlette in the early part of 1844, and held the office until the close of the year 1850, when he died. He was a man of strong, mind, quick perception, impulsive and liberal. He gathered the strong points in a case quicker than any lawyer I ever knew. If there was the least fraud or usury in the transactions involved, he was sure to scent it. He illustrated in a high degree the truth of the saying that the character of the lawyer's practice before he goes on the Bench, has a modifying influence on his opinions and rulings as a Judge. Judge Cahal's practice had been largely on the defensive side of suits and as a Judge instead of trying to aid every one that came into Court, to get what they wanted, his mind was active to discover whether they did not want something they ought not to have, and if they did not come into his Court with absolutely clean hands, they were turned out. Widow women and children, needed no solicitors in his Court. He guarded well their interests. I beg leave to relate an instance in this respect. The Administrators of a deceased man filed a Bill to sell a small portion of the land to pay debts. They believed the state was solvent. Before the land was sold the estate proved to be insolvent. The Administrators, with the widow, applied for a sale of the whole tract; the widow saying she desired her husband's debts paid, if it took all the land. The Judge promptly refused to order a sale. The widow then executed a deed, relinquishing dower, etc. and her deed was presented to the Judge with the Bill.

The Judge in a stern and very emphatic manner told the lawyer who had charge of the Bill that the widow's dower should not be sold; that he knew what was best for her, better than she did herself, and ordered her dower to be laid off. The woman was greatly displeased at the time, but two years after she said, Judge Cahal was the best friend she had ever had. As a Chancellor his opinions were rarely reversed.

Honorable A. O. P. Nicholson, of Columbia, succeeded Cahal by appointment from the Governor in the early part of 1851. He held the office a few months and resigned. His distinguished abilities as a Judge and as a statesman, and his great worth as a man are so well known to the people of Giles County, that I can add nothing that could interest.

Honorable Samuel D. Frierson, of Columbia, succeeded Nicholson by appointment from the Governor in the Summer of 1851. He held the office only a few months until it was filled by the Legislature.

John S. Brien, of Davidson County, succeeded Frierson. He was elected Oct. 24, 1851, and entered on the duties of his office the eighth of March 1852. His first Court was at Pulaski at that date when his Commission was spread on the minutes. Judge Brien held the office about two years and resigned—the date of his resignation cannot be ascertained. He was a good lawyer, an able advocate and popular with the people. As a Chancellor his decisions were very seldom reversed; and while on the Bench he was courteous to the bar, to suitors, and all having business in Court, and it may be well said, he was a popular Chancellor.

Samuel D. Frierson succeeded Brien and held the office until his death the elevnth of March 1866. He possessed a clear, discriminating mind, was always calm and self-possessed, patient and respectful. He was the only Judge I ever knew on the Bench but what I could tell before a case was half through, from something he said, his manner, look, or tone of voice, on which side his mind was unconsciously drifting. This I regard as the highest and rarest qualification of a Judge. He possessed another rare qualification in a high degree; that of being able to correct his own opinions, when once formed, by patient, laborious, investigation, without any extraneous influences, brought to bear on him. Altogether he was a model Chancellor. I cannot forego the pleasure of relating an incident illustrative of his character as a Judge. Soon after he went on the Bench a suit between two preachers was decided by him. From the record neither had acted in perfect good faith and the conduct of both as shown by the pleadings and proof, was open to criticism. After deciding the cause the Judge went on to speak of the want of good faith in the losing party. When the lawyer on that side told the Judge his client was a minister of the gospel, he was very much surprised and apologized, and as a sort of relief to the lawyer and the friends of his client if any were present, he animadverted with some severity on the successful party; when his lawyer got up and told the Judge his client was also a minister of the Gospel. The Judge, more surprised and mortified than before, again apologized. He then told the bar that his indiscretions that day should be a lesson to him. That in the future he would confine himself strictly to a decision of the questions involved in the controversy, without reference to the motives and moral delinquencies of the parties—farther than was necessary in his decision; and whatever might be his own opinions, he would keep them to himself. I never knew him to depart from the rule then prescribed.

SHERIFFS

Charles Neely was the first Sheriff of the County, elected by the County Court the third Monday in February, 1810. He held the office only a short time and resigned.

Jas Buford, who was deputy under Neely was elected in his place. The date is not know but probably in the Summer or Fall of 1810.   He held the office until March, 1814. James Buford came to the County in the Fall of 1807, was a prominent and influential citizen, a successful farmer, was twice elected Representative from this County to the Legislature, and was long a member of the Baptist Church. He died in 1845.

Maxmillian H. Buchanan succeeded Buford. Was elected in March, 1814, and held the office until about 1818. He was one among the very first settlers, coming in the Summer or Fall of 1807. He was one of the first Justices of the Peace in the County, and assisted in organizing the County Court, and electing County officers the third Monday in February, 1810. He removed to Lawrence County soon after that County was established; and was long a prominent and influential citizen of that county. From thence he removed to the State of Mississippi. He was born in Union District, S. C., October 10th, 1783, and died January, 1858.

Jas. Perry who was a deputy under Buchanan, succeeded him and held the office until about 1824. He was an energetic and efficient public officer, and a man of considerable influence in the County.

Lewis H. Brown succeeded Perry and held the office until the latter part of 1831. He was well qualified for the office and was a popular sheriff.

Thos. C. Porter succeeded Brown in November, 1831. He was one of the early settlers of the County. His father came in 1808 and settled near Mount Moriah. Thos. C. Porter was a very popular man and was a member of the Constitutional Convention in 1834 from the counties of Giles and Lincoln. He held the office until the Spring of 1836, when the officers elected under the new Constitution went into office.

Thos. S. Webb succeeded Porter by the election of the people in March 1836, and enterd on the duties of the office shortly after. He held the office six years and was a competent and faithful officer.

John A. Jackson succeeded Webb in the Spring of 1842, and held the office for six years. He was an efficient, faithful and popular sheriff. He was born near Hillsboro, N. C., February 15th, 1805, and died January 18th, 1869, in the faith; and with the Christian hope.

Amasa Ezell succeeded Jackson in the Spring of 1848, and held the office two years. He had been an officer for many years, had served as deputy sheriff six years; and was thought to be better acquainted with the duties and responsibilities of the office than any man who had filled it. He was a competent, efficient and faithful officer. He was born in Union District in 1806, or 1807, and died August 11th, 1856, aged about 49 years. He was for many years a member of the Baptist Church; and was a consistent and exemplary Christian.

Jas. D. Goodman succeeded Ezell in the Spring of 1850, and held the office four years. He was a competent and faithful officer.

Joshua Morris succeeded Goodman in the Spring of 1854, and held the office two years. He was a competent, energetic, and faithful public officer, a man of property and influence, and still lives, honored and respected by all who know him.

John Kouns succeeded Mooris in the Spring of 1856, and held the office until the Courts were closed by the Civil War. He was kind and obliging as a man and as an officer, and discharged his duties faithfully.

REGISTERS

Jesse Westmoreland was the first Register of the County He was elected the third Monday in Feb. 1810, at the organiza tion of the County Court. He settled the place now owned by Jno. Newbill, five miles South-east of Pulaski He lived only a few years after his appointment and for several months before his death he was absent from the County seeking medical aid and died in Davidson County. It is not certainly known who succeeded him. The records of the County Court have been destroyed. The well known hand-writing of Fountain Lester, who was Register for many years, first appears on the Register's books July 11, 1814, and continues on from that time. Whether he succeeded West-moreland or some other Register after him cannot be ascer-tained.

The recording is in several different hand-writings, be-tween the early entries of Westmoreland, and the commence ment of Lester's. I have an impression that Somerset Moore, who was one of the first Justices of the County, held the of-fice a short time. He died a few years after the County was organized. Whether any person held the office between Westmoreland and Lester is not known.

Fountain Lester, as already stated, discharged the duties of the office in July 1814, and held the office until the early part of 1836. He was a competent and faithful Register, and held the office longer than any other man since his day.

Daniel McCormack succeeded Lester by election of the people, under provisions of the Constitution of 1834, and held the office four years.

P. T. L. McCanless succeeded McCormack in April 1840, and held the office until his death in the Summer or Fall of 1853.

Andrew Fay succeeded McCanless by election of the of County at October term 1853, and held the office until the 6th of April, 1854.

Daniel G. Anderson succeeded Fay in 1854, and held the office until the officers elected under the provisions of the Constitution of 1870, went into office. He was in the office longer than any other officer except Lester. He was a competent and faithful Register. He died a few years ago—the date of death I have not before me.

REPRESENTATIVES AND SENATORS

Representatives and Senators in the Legislature of Tennessee, together with the Districts embracing Giles County to-wit:

Senators—Williamson and Rutherford, Maury and Bedford, embracing Giles and Lincoln. 1809 Thomas H. Benton, 1811 Newton Cannon. Giles and Lincoln—1813 (Not given), 1815 George Coulter, 1817 George Coulter, 1819 Wm. Edmiston, 1821 Aaron V. Brown, 1823 Aaron V. Brown, 1825 William E. Kennedy (resigned in 1826 and Aaron V. Brown elected for call session in 1826.) 1827 A. V. Brown, 1829 Isaac Holeman, 1831 William H. Field, 1833 William Moore, 1835 William Moore, 1837 Jas. Caruthers, 1839 George W. Jones, 1841 William T. Ross.

Representatives—Williamson and Maury embracing Giles 1809 William Frierson, 1811 Amos Johnson. Giles alone— 1813 (Not given) 1815 John Clack, 1817 John Dickey, 1819

John Clack, 1821 John H. Camp, 1823 John Clack, 1825 John
H. Camp, 1827 John H. Camp, 1829 Thomas K. Gordon, 1831
Aaron V. Brown, 1833 E. J. Shields, 1835 Thos. K. Gordon and
James Buchanan, 1837 Neill S. Brown, William R. Brown,
1839 Jas. Buford and Jno. Buchanan, 1841 Jas. Buford and
Jno. Buchanan.

Under the new apportionment Giles elected one member,
and Giles and Lincoln Floater, and Giles and Maury a Senator
Senators—Giles and Maury: 1843 A. O. P. Nicholson, 1845
Jonas E. Thomas, 1847 Thomas M. Jones, 1849 R. A. L. Wilkes
1851 Ephraim H. Osborne.

Representative and Floater—1843 John W. Goode; Rob-
ert Farquaharson, Floater; 1845 John Buchanan; T. M. Jones,
Floater; 1847 Archibald Wright; Jno. M. Bright, Floater; 1849
Thos. Buford; Nathan Adams, Floater; 1851 R. M. Bugg; Jno.
McDaniel, Floater.

Under the apportionment of 1851, Lincoln, Marshall and
Giles send Floater; and Giles, Lawrence and Wayne, Senator.

Senator—1853 George H. Nixon, 1855 Thomas J. Brown,
1857 Thomas J. Brown, 1859 W. H. Hunter, 1861 F. L. Wilson.

Representatives—1853 T. Buford, Wm. B. Chambliss
Floater, 1855 R. H. Watkins, H. N. Cowden, Floater, 1857 E.
E. Harney, Jas. M. Davidson, Floater, 1859 Jo J. Beaty, Thos.
J. Kennedy Floater, 1861 James McCallum, Jno. Laws, Floater

Senators and Representatives in Congress from Tennessee, the District embracing the County of Giles, from its organization to the late war. In the appointment of Representatives, under the census of 1800, Tennessee was entitled to
three Representatives: I have not access to the records of the
Legislature districting the state, and as I therefor may be
mistaken in the number of our district, I will give the ones
I believe represented our district.   Commencing with the
Tenth Congress, October the 26th, 1807.

Senators—10th Congress, 1807—Joseph Anderson, Daniel
Smith, 11th Congress, 1809—John Smith, (Smith resigned in
1807) Joseph Anderson, 12th Congress, 1811—Geo. W. Campbell, (Not given.)

Representatives—10 Congress, 1807—Geo. W. Campbell,
Jesse Wharton, John Rhea.   11th Congress, 1809—Robert

Weakley, Pleasant M. Miller, John Rhea. 12th Congress, 1811 Felix Grundy, John Sevier, John Rhea.

In the apportionment under the census of 1810, Tennessee was entitled to six Representatives. The State was re-districted by the session of the Legislature in 1812; the journals of which (the only source of information to which I have access), do not show the Counties composing the several districts; but from an amendment offered by Mr. Cannon on the third reading of the Bill, it appears that Davidson and Williamson were in the fifth district, and Maury and Giles in the sixth. I will therefore give the names of the members I suppose represented our district.

Senators—13th Congress, 1813—Joseph Anderson, George W. Campbell, (Campbell resigned in 1818 succeeded by J. W. Eaton. 14th Congress, 1815—George W. Campbell, John Williamson. 15th Congress, 1817—George W. Campbell, John Williams, (Campbell resigned in 1818, J. H. Eaton appointed) 16th Congress, 1819—J. H. Eaton, John Williams. 17th Congress, 1821—John H. Eaton, Jno. Williams.

Representatives—13th Congress, 1813—P. W. Humphreys. 14th Congress, 1815—Isaacs Thomas. 15th Congress, 1817— Geo. W. L. Marr. 16th Congress, 1819—Henry H. Bryan. 17th Congress, 1821—Henry H. Bryan.

18th Congress. In the opportionment under the census of 1820, Tennessee was entitled to nine Representatives; the State was re-districted by the call session of the Legislature of 1822, in which Maury, Bedford, Lincoln and Giles, composed one district.

Senators—18th Congress, 1823—John H. Eaton, Andrew Jackson. 19th Congress, 1825—John H. Eaton, Andrew Jackson. 20th Congress, 1927—John H. Eaton, Hugh L. White. 21st Congress, 1829—John H. Eaton, Hugh L. White. 22nd Congress, 1831—Felix Grundy, Hugh L. White.

Representatives—18th Congress, 1823—James T. Stanford 19th Congress, 1825—James K. Polk. 20th Congress, 1827— James K. Polk. 21st Congress, 1829—James K. Polk. 22nd Congress 1831—James K. Polk..

23rd Congress, 1833—In the apportionment under the census of 1830, Tennessee was entitled to thirteen Representatives. The State was re-districted by the call session of 1832, in which Lincoln, Giles, Lawrence and Wayne comprised one district.

Senators—23rd Congress, 1833—Felix Grundy, H. L. White. 24th Congress, 1835—F. Grundy, H. L. White.

Representatives—23rd Congress, 1833 William M. Inge. 24th Congress, 1835—Ebenezer J. Shields. 25th Congress, 1837—E. J. Shields. 26th Congress, 1839—Aaron V. Brown. 27th Congress, 1841—Aaron V. Brown.

In the apportionment under the census of 1840, Tennessee was entitled to ———— Repreesntatives. In re-districting the State, Maury, Giles, Lawrence, Wayne and Hickman were in the same district.

Representatives—28th Congress, 1843—A. V. Brown. 29th Congress, 1845—Barclay Martin. 30th Congress, 1847—James H. Thomas. 31st Congress, 1849—J. H. Thomas. 32nd Congress, 1851—William H. Polk.

In the apportionment under the census of 1850, in re-districting the State, Giles, Lawrence, Wayne, Henderson were in the same district.

Representatives—33rd Congress, 1853—Robert M. Bugg. 34th Congress, 1855—John V. Wright. 35th Congress, 1857—John V. Wright. 36th Congress, 1859—John V. Wright. John V. Wright's last term expired March the 4th, 1861, after which Tennessee joined the Southern Confederacy.

MILITIA OFFICERS

For twenty years or more after the County was organized, the militia was mustered and drilled. Militia officers were deemed honorable and the offices were sought for by the best men of the County.

The first Regiment organized was the Thirty-seventh and embraced the whole County. Robert Steele was the first Colonel, and Claiborne McVey and James Buford the first Majors.

After the war of 1812, the regiment was divided, and a new Regiment, the Fifty-second was formed of the Northern half of the County. This left Pulaski with the old Regiment.

Thos. K. Gordon was the first Colonel elected in the new Regiment and Richard H. Allen and James Simmons the Majors.

After the division, James Terrell was elected Colonel of the old Regiment and Thos. Wilkerson and William Rose, Majors.

After Col. Terrell moved from the County about 1821, Wlliam Rose was unanimously elected Colonel, and Gilliam Harwell and Abel Wilson, Majors. About 1825, there was a reorganization of the militia and another Regiment formed, embracing the North-western part of the County, including Pulaski. Richard H. Allen was the first Colonel of the Regiment last formed. Simpson H. White, Lieut. Col., and John H. Rivers and Edmund Tipton, Majors.

David Gordon was elected Colonel of Gordon's old Regiment, embracing the North-eastern part of the County. Joseph Nance, Lieutenant-Colonel; William Shields and Lewis B. Marks, Majors.

In the reorganization the 37th or the old Regiment, embraced the Southern part of the County; extending across the country from East to West. Gilliam Harwell was elected Colonel, Gustin Kearney, Lieutenant-Colonel, Edward A. Dillon and Claiborne Kyle, Majors.

On the death of Dillon and resignation of Kearney the next year, Claiborne Kyle was elected Lieutenant-Colonel, and Wm. H. Moore and Jefferson Kyle, Mayors. On the removal of Kyle and Moore in 1829, Dr. W. E. Harold was elected Lieutenant-Colonel, and Patrick H. Braden, Major. After these, several prominent and influential men were from time to time elected officers of the militia. But about 1829 or 1830, the interest in military offices began to decline.

Until the adoption of the new Consitution, in 1834, the election or appointment of justices of the peace was regulated by Captain's Companies or "Beats," as it is now, by Civil Districts.

WRIGHT'S
  JOHN V, 124

-Y-

YANCEY
  TRYON M, 97
  TRYON M., 16
YANCY
  TRYON M., 27, 28
YARD
  COURT HOUSE, 110
  KIRK'S, 108
YERGER
  JOHN K, 97
YOIKLEY
  ANDREW, 31
YOKLEY
  ANDREW, 14, 21, 30
YOUNG
  ARCHIBALD, 38
  JOHN, 37, 38

-Z-

ZEALNOR
  ARNOLD, 41(2), 75

www.ingramcontent.com/pod-product-compliance
Lightning Source LLC
Chambersburg PA
CBHW080616270326
41928CB00016B/3090